RESOURCE BOOKS FOR TEACHERS

series editor
ALAN MALEY

PRONUNCIATION

Clement Laroy

Oxford University Press

Oxford University Press
Walton Street, Oxford OX2 6DP

Oxford   New York
Athens   Auckland   Bangkok   Bombay
Calcutta   Cape Town   Dar es Salaam   Delhi
Florence   Hong Kong   Istanbul   Karachi
Kuala Lumpur   Madras   Madrid   Melbourne
Mexico City   Nairobi   Paris   Singapore
Taipei   Tokyo   Toronto

and associated companies in
Berlin   Ibadan

Oxford and *Oxford English* are trade marks of
Oxford University Press

ISBN 0 19 437087 9

© Oxford University Press 1995

First published 1995
Second impression 1996

The right of Clement Laroy to be identified as author of this
work has been asserted by him in accordance with the Copyright
Designs and Patents Act 1988.

Set by Wyvern Typesetting Ltd, Bristol.

Printed in Hong Kong.

Acknowledgements

I would like to thank the PE teacher who more than thirty years ago pointed out to me that learning is not exclusively a rational process.

Heartfelt thanks to all my students from all over the world who, over many years, have made me think, provided feedback, and tried out the ideas and exercises in this book. Without their criticism and their trust, this book would not have been written. In particular, I wish to thank my students in Zaire, as well as Vinh Đinh, Quôc-Nhân, Myriam, Véronique, Renato, Nathalie, and Sonia.

I need to express my deep gratitude to David Cranmer: his friendship, coaching, and encouragements have been crucial.

The following friends and colleagues have helped in various ways—often unknown to them: Joan Agosta (USA/France), colleagues and friends from the Athénée Warocquez in Morlanwelz (Belgium), Jean Auquier (Belgium), Ruth Baratz (Israel), Joseph Cocchio (Belgium), Elena De Ru (Holland), Edouard Desmed (Belgium), Bernard Dufeu (France/Germany), Seth Lindstromberg (USA/UK), John Morgan (UK), Mario Rinvolucri (UK), and Marco Saerens (Université Libre de Bruxelles, Belgium).

I owe a lot to my wife and children; their patience and their uninhibited criticism have helped me to go further and to probe more deeply.

Finally, a special word of thanks to the team from Oxford University Press. Grateful thanks to Alan Maley for his support and his valuable advice and suggestions, to Anne Conybeare for her encouragement to write this book, and to Julia Sallabank for her thorough and sympathetic editing.

For my parents

Contents

1 Tuning in to the language

3 Approaching speech sounds

The author and series editor

During a career spanning more than thirty years, **Clement Laroy** has taught in secondary schools in Belgium and in Africa, worked for educational television (Scientific and Technical English), worked in the Department of Applied Linguistics at the University of Brussels (Institut de Phonétique), taught young children, and trained staff in companies. Since 1975 he has been a teacher trainer. He is also a trainer at ISC St Louis College for Business Studies in Brussels. He has published several articles and is co-author with David Cranmer of *Musical Openings: Using Music in the Language Classroom* (Pilgrims-Longman, 1992) and has contributed to the *The Standby Book*, edited by Seth Lindstromberg (Cambridge University Press, forthcoming).

Alan Maley worked for The British Council from 1962 to 1988, serving as English Language Officer in Yugoslavia, Ghana, Italy, France, and China, and as Regional Representative in South India (Madras). From 1988 to 1993 he was Director-General of the Bell Educational Trust, Cambridge. He is currently Senior Fellow in the Department of English Language and Literature of the National University of Singapore. He has written *Literature*, in this series, *Beyond Words*, *Sounds Interesting*, *Sounds Intriguing*, *Words*, *Variations on a Theme*, and *Drama Techniques in Language Learning* (all with Alan Duff), *The Mind's Eye* (with Françoise Grellet and Alan Duff), *Learning to Listen* and *Poem into Poem* (with Sandra Moulding), and *Short and Sweet*. He is also Series Editor for the Oxford Supplementary Skills series.

Foreword

This book bears witness to the renewed interest in the teaching of pronunciation. It is interesting to note that pronunciation has been relatively neglected in recent years—many courses do not deal with it specifically at all, preferring to leave it to a process of osmosis—yet most learners attach great importance to it. The way we sound when we speak a foreign language has a strong influence on the assumptions other people make about us and the judgements they make about the sort of people we are. Our pronunciation is also intimately connected with our feelings about ourselves: our confidence (or lack of it), our sense of identity, and our self-esteem.

This book starts from the premiss that, when dealing with pronunciation, what goes on inside our heads (and our hearts) is at least as important as what we do with our mouths. It has been customary to present pronunciation work in an atomistic, analytical, and segregated way. Here by contrast the approach is holistic, synthesizing, and integrative. It is holistic in that it involves both physical and personality factors. It is synthesizing in that emphasis is placed on suprasegmental features such as rhythm and stress rather than on isolated phonemic features. It is integrative in that it places pronunciation work in the framework of other language learning activities, rather than separating it off completely.

This selection of highly original activities therefore works to lower the learners' threshold of resistance to the foreign-ness of the foreign language and to create positive attitudes, both to the language and to their own ability to handle it. It works largely by 'aiming off for wind', using holistic activities involving relaxation, rhythm, music, and physical movement as a way of approaching pronunciation obliquely, rather than confronting it head-on. It presents, in short, a radical alternative to the teaching of pronunciation as previously conceived. It will be invaluable to all those teachers looking for ways to 'help their learners learn the unteachable'.

Alan Maley

The English language
is
a kingdom
and
a sleeping beauty.

You must
awaken her
in yourself,
and the whole kingdom
will come to life
and be
yours.

L. L. Szkutnik

Introduction

'The road is difficult, not because of the deep river and the high mountains that bar the way, but because we lose heart when we think of the river and the mountain.'

Vietnamese saying

When I was a young, inexperienced teacher, I was convinced that English pronunciation was exceptionally difficult, especially for speakers of some languages. But I believed that all the problems could be solved by phonetics. So I decided to take the bull by the horns.

I used to begin courses by teaching the names of the speech organs and the difference between vowels and consonants. My learners also practised reading and writing texts written in phonemic script.

As a consequence my classes 'knew all about' the uvula and lip rounding; they practised minimal pairs, prominence, and intonation nuclei and contours; they had a lot of dictations and repeated a lot; and yet, what I viewed as *the* formula for teaching English pronunciation did not yield the results I and my learners had hoped for, in spite of all our hard work.

I kept faith and hope, followed new trends, disguised drills as games to make them more palatable, was seduced by communicative approaches—and never let go. And yet, with many learners the results were still disappointing.

I gradually realized that phonetics and drills often led learners to hate or fear the study of English and inhibited their speaking. With many learners it was hard to see the link between class practice and progress. I would also come across people from language backgrounds which have a reputation for finding the pronunciation of English particularly arduous who had overcome the obstacles.

All this suggested to me that it is not simply the intrinsic difficulty of English that causes many students to stumble and struggle with pronunciation. I thought it might be useful to try to understand what the obstacles are, how pronunciation is learned, and what conditions help learners internalize it.

Having lost my youthful certainties, I gradually came to a number of conclusions. These did not constitute the ingredients of a new 'magical formula', but they did engender activities which turned out to be fun while giving learners insights and helping them.

Here, then, are some of the results of my observations.

Historical obstacles

Our affective links with our mother tongue are normally positive and strong, but when we learn a foreign language we have a history and prejudices to contend with, and the older we get, the more intrusive this history is likely to become. Think of all the countries and peoples who have had contact with people speaking various brands of English during wars, or who were once part of the British Empire. Others may resent what they see as the inroads English (in any of its varieties) has made as a world lingua franca. Such negative feelings can produce a strong desire to set oneself apart from the language and its native speakers. After all, even within the English-speaking world people keep themselves apart regionally and socially through the way they pronounce the language.

Personal and sociological obstacles

A person will only want to achieve something if they believe it is achievable and worth attaining because of the social, intellectual, or aesthetic benefits it will bring. Many factors may interfere with learners' setting and attaining their goals.

First, learners' relationships with the smaller or wider community around them have a strong influence on their desire or unwillingness to learn a foreign language well. Here are some examples.

– Adolescents, for example, may actively try not to be good in order to integrate better with their peers, and may wish to set themselves off from their teachers who would like them to take on a standard British English pronunciation. They themselves may feel more attracted by the English spoken by members of their favourite pop group or by Americans, Australians, or Indians.

– Immigrants to non-English-speaking countries may want to achieve a very good pronunciation, to set themselves off from, or even above, the nationals of their adopted—or imposed—country.

– Others, by contrast, may want to keep a pronunciation that clearly shows their origins. The most extreme case of this that I have come across is that of a third-generation Italian immigrant in a non-English-speaking country who spoke English with a very strong Italian accent. He also used a lot of Italian body language when he spoke English. None of this happened when he spoke the language of the area he lived in. He eventually said he wanted everyone to know he was proud of his Italian origins and that he felt that in this way he was avenging the treatment his grandfather had suffered when he had first arrived to work in the coal mines, even though he had no particular reason to take it out on English.

Such extreme cases are enlightening as they demonstrate indisputably that language learning is the focal point of strong emotions. They tell us this dimension cannot be ignored in our class work with all learners, especially when the problems are less obvious. The way learners speak is an expression of their identity. We need to respect their choice of a non-standard accent provided they are made aware that it carries potential public disadvantages (such as the risk of being misunderstood), as well as very real personal advantages.

Second, the question of what may happen to the learners' personal identity when they have to produce the unfamiliar sounds of a foreign language may be important. One of my students once put it like this: 'What is to become of our personality if we acquire an English intonation?'

This leads us to another important point. Not only will it be almost impossible for teachers to get their learners to pronounce better than the learners themselves want to, but it will be equally difficult to get them to become better than they believe they can be, even if they need to in order to get a diploma or succeed in their job.

What makes learners believe they will not be able to pronounce English well?

People from some language backgrounds think it is unimaginable for people from their culture to pronounce English well, and this is often reinforced by prejudices and stereotypes. For example, Scandinavian and Dutch people are often presented as people who can achieve a good English accent, while speakers of Romance languages are supposed not to be able to. The differences that contrastive studies bring to light between the mother tongue and English will only reinforce this conviction, even in teachers. This can adversely affect the development of learners from these countries, even if they come across people who prove the contrary. Though there may be some apparently objective reasons for the learners' problems, they do not provide sufficient explanation for the lack of success. Near-similarity can be just as much a problem as great differences. In the end, the most important single factor is the learners themselves.

Another common belief, which is sometimes presented as an axiom of psychology, is that after a certain age good pronunciation of a foreign language can no longer be achieved.

This is sometimes called the 'critical period', seen as either around the age of seven or eight, or puberty. Many adults are convinced that 'at their age' the only thing they can hope for is to manage to survive in a foreign language.

Whatever truth there may be in this, it is also true that many people who start learning a foreign language after the 'critical period' manage to achieve excellent pronunciation. The problems of those who appear to be incapable of doing so may simply be due to the self-consciousness that comes with age and not to age itself.

Adolescents, for example, often feel ridiculous producing 'strange' sounds, or they may feel they look awful. This inhibits them; they avoid speaking and cannot develop a frame of mind that allows them to use their full potential. As the years go by they become convinced that for them 'English is simply impossible to pronounce'.

Adult students may notice younger students succeeding where they have not, and feel that they are 'losing face' in front of younger colleagues.

So teachers are up against strong resistance, prejudice, myth, and a belief that all efforts will be hopeless.

All these factors have led me to the conclusion that problems like these—and there can be as many different and compounded problems as there are learners—need to be tackled in order to help learners with pronunciation.

This book, then, does not give a description of the pronunciation of English. It does not provide traditional drills on suprasegmental features or phonemes. Instead, it shows ways to overcome obstacles to good pronunciation that can be applied whatever the mother tongue of the learners.

The approach used in this book

1 An oblique approach

I believe that much of the teaching and improvement of pronunciation should be indirect. Teachers need to know what they are teaching, but the learners need not always be aware of what they are learning. This will not only avoid arousing immediate resistance, but can also reduce self-consciousness.

This approach on its own is very often enough to produce considerable improvement, or at least create a state of mind where the learners can benefit from other pronunciation work. If you are going to give explicit explanation and correction, it should be when students can really benefit from it. This requires patience and empathy. Through careful observation the teacher must detect which learners need reassurance above all, and which ones are ready to try to improve. If the students ask for explanation, it probably means they are ready for some analysis. This may be the time to provide descriptions of the intonational system or the position of the speech organs for certain sounds, or to do traditional activities such as 'minimal pair' practice.

2 A pragmatic approach

The activities do not aim to fit any particular description of English pronunciation. Descriptions of the language can never satisfy every individual user; as with maps, getting somewhere may mean taking a route not shown. Often, by asking learners to do one thing, we actually get them to achieve another—the activities must be seen as steps in a process.

3 A holistic approach

The learners' personalities

Pronunciation cannot be separated from the people who speak the language, nor cut off from the rest of language and learning in general. It follows that deeper contact with the language and opportunities to think and feel in it are probably of most help to students in improving their pronunciation. This means that many aspects of the learners' personalities must be involved, for example, the need to become aware of, and to deal with, any grudges they may have. They may need to accept that they are not betraying their group, culture, country, ancestors, or themselves if they pronounce English well. If they free themselves from the burden of the past they can then come to experience sounding English or American as something desirable and achievable.

Enhancing learner confidence

Make sure your learners feel you expect them to succeed, and that the process need not be arduous.

It is important that they themselves should decide how far they want to go in integrating with the target language. They should always be involved in the process of setting their personal agenda for development.

It is also essential not to view scope for improvement as symptoms of weakness, and difficulties as a crime against the language. This means that repetitive correction should be banned, for there is no reason to believe that what does not work once will work better by being repeated. Creating a relaxed atmosphere where learners can approach pronunciation and the language in general in an uninhibited way is crucial. This should allow learners who have developed a feeling of inadequacy to discover the language anew. Games, group dynamics, relaxation, and other activities which loosen up the learners foster an atmosphere where experimentation is not viewed as threatening.

Using all the learners' senses

Approaching pronunciation holistically means addressing all the learners' senses as well as their feelings and aesthetic perception. A comparison with music would be that their instruments have to be tuned, but that their minds also have to be alert and in harmony.

The activities lead learners to listen and speak with all their senses, so the 'sound of English' is associated with what they can see, hear, taste, and feel physically and emotionally. In this way they are led to discover the beauty of the sound of the language they are learning.

This approach is a natural one and is in accordance with research which shows that better learning takes place when all the senses are activated, leading learners to initiate new learning strategies (Williams 1983; Stein and Meredith 1993).

Approaching pronunciation

Babies start with the potential for learning any language, but gradually we become attuned to our mother tongue and tend to hear everything under its influence. We need to learn to perceive the sound of a new language in its own right, as if we were hearing it, like babies, for the first time. This can be done with the help of electronic equipment (Tomatis 1963, 1975; Molholt 1988; Anderson-Hsieh 1992), but this approach—apart from not being generally available—might be felt to be too mechanical.

Relaxation is a very useful tool to help learners leave the rest of the world behind, reactivate their sense of discovery, investigate a new world of sounds, and mobilize all their resources. It also improves articulation and voice quality.

Several activities in this book approach pronunciation through music. There are obvious parallels between music and language: both use rhythm and pitch changes to express meaning. Music plays with sounds to produce pleasure, helps to overcome self-consciousness, and can activate other abilities which can in turn help to activate linguistic capacity. Suggestions are made as to what kind of music to use, but choose music your students will respond to easily for a start, expanding your selection as you go, catering for all your students and opening up their sonic world and their minds.

Learners are also encouraged to experiment with their voices as the gate to non-analytical learning skills is opened.

All this should lead to a more intimate and deeper approach as well as a better understanding of the language in general.

How to use this book

Varieties of English

If possible, it is best to allow your learners to choose the variety they prefer; this fundamental choice can be very important. In this book, what is said applies to any variety of what is usually called 'English'; please add whatever adjective you like before it (American, Australian, or Canadian, for example). In the examples I have used standard English and received (British) pronunciation as a basis, but you can easily provide a parallel example that suits your situation.

Using phonemic script

Should you use phonemic script? It depends on the learners you are dealing with. With young learners do not use it at all— associate the pronunciation with key words they can pronounce well (for example, teach them to pronounce 'low' and 'road' like 'no'). Associating sounds and their spellings in this way should be a regular feature of your classes once reading and writing are introduced. If your learners have to be able to look up the pronunciation of words they have never heard in dictionaries, gradually associate the key words with the phonemic symbols as and when needed.

Adapting to your learners

Age

You will find suggestions in the text, but your own judgement will be essential, for example in choosing appropriate texts. Here are some general principles.

Activities that require life experience or adult thinking will have to be reduced or totally omitted with young learners. If they cannot write yet, use pictures and drawings or simplify the activity so that it can be done orally.

If, on the other hand, an activity strikes you as being too childish for your learners, think about how to make it acceptable. Explaining the benefits they can derive from an activity is often sufficient to obtain their collaboration. Do not give up in advance, and *persevere*. Inability to play and reluctance to allow the child in themselves to express itself is often a symptom of the very rigidity that is an obstacle to their improvement.

Level

Most of the activities can be done at all levels. Activities which introduce aspects of pronunciation can be used for revision or improvement if your learners are more advanced. A few activities cannot be done with beginners, but in most cases dealing with beginners simply means you have to use the learners' mother tongue for some explanations, or choose a text they can manage.

How much pronunciation work should you do?

Pronunciation should always be at the back of your mind. Be ready to steer your learners when necessary, and weave the activities into the fabric of your lessons. Many of the activities in the book make excellent 'warmers' and only take 5 to 10 minutes. It is important that you do not allow mistakes to become fossilized with beginners, but correcting too much and too overtly is counter-productive.

Involve your learners

Pronunciation is not something the teacher can instil in learners; it is something the learners assimilate for themselves. As a teacher you are the initiator, but respect your learners' choices and encourage them to have a personal agenda for development and to express their feelings. Develop their autonomy by suggesting they can and should work on their own, at home and in the wider world. Finally, welcome initiative and listen carefully to any ideas they may have about their progress.

Choosing activities

The order in which activities appear in the book is based on a progression, but you need to be alert to the needs of your class to decide what to work on next. You may need to move backwards and forwards between chapters, working on awareness, rhythm, intonation, or sounds, coming back when learners have absorbed a new feature. Try to maintain a sense of progression. Suggestions for this can be found in the activities.

Using the activities

The activities are devised as self-contained units. Most take only a little class time, but full benefit will only really be gained if they are repeated at intervals or followed up in the ways suggested as well as in ways that you will think of as a result of what you notice in class. As many provide useful conversation or listening activities, they can easily be integrated into other lessons.

If activities of this kind are a new way of working for you and your class, first choose the ones you feel most comfortable with and progressively experiment with others.

Often it is suggested that you do some relaxation first. This is very important as tension prevents learners from benefiting from the activity, while relaxation improves articulation and voice quality, and allows learners to discover unexpected potential. You will find suggestions for relaxation exercises in 1.1, but you can of course use other forms of relaxation that you and your students are comfortable with.

Music and songs are an integral part of the approach. Do not worry about your and your students' musical abilities. If you are not brilliant this will give courage to your less musical students. If you feel really insecure, use a recording but sing along with the class. Students who are not very musical will be carried along by the group and will progressively gain confidence and sing better.

Conclusion

If you feel you have too little time to do pronunciation exercises, consider that most of the activities in this book are short and can be integrated with other work in class. Most of them are simple and fun. You will probably find that 10 minutes spent on one of these at the beginning of or during a lesson will not only result in a great improvement in your learners' pronunciation, but will also have a positive effect on their attitude to the language and how they relate to the group.

This book is a starting point for both learners and teachers. The activities should provide openings that will lead learners and teachers to discover or invent new angles that are better adapted to their own language experience.

1 Tuning in to the language

As I mentioned in the general introduction, it is crucial for learners to build up a positive relationship with the language and its speakers. They need to gain confidence and get used to looking and sounding different. The activities in this chapter help them achieve this by gradually 'tuning in' to the language and developing a good relationship with it.

Activities 1.1 to 1.5 should help to dismantle any historical and personal barriers there may be between the learners and the language.

The learners need to discover a different sound environment where they will later progressively recognize and distinguish between sounds they cannot differentiate at first. For this they need to be aware of how they perceive the target language (1.6). Other activities in Chapters 2, 3, and 4 build on this.

Since producing sounds is intimately linked with our bodies, the way we breathe, and the way we use our muscles, it must have an influence on the way we feel and the way we look. The rest of this chapter gradually introduces the learners to these aspects.

All the activities aim to foster learner confidence. Increased awareness helps them to come to terms with what may hinder their development, and to use their learning potential to better effect.

1.1 Relaxing to learn

LEVEL	**All**
TIME	**2–20 minutes**
AIMS	**Inducing a state of mind that facilitates learning; improving articulation and voice quality**
PROCEDURE	**A Sitting comfortably**

If your students are sitting at desks, ask them to sit with their backs touching the back of their chairs, resting their feet flat, somewhat apart, on the floor. Their arms should rest on the desk. The most relaxing position would be to lie on the floor (if you have space), with legs extended and the arms alongside the body, the palms of the hands on the floor.

B Relaxing

To relax deeply, follow the procedure below. It is based on Schultz's autogenic training (Schultz 1956; Malfait 1980; Kermani 1992). Speak in a calm and slow voice, not too loudly. Observe the class to check that everyone is getting progressively more relaxed—you can tell from their breathing. Progressively synchronize your breathing and that of the group. Pause for the time it takes to breathe slowly in and out. Speak as you breathe out, and slow down if necessary.

1 Say the following, adapting it if necessary to your students' level or if they are lying down. If they are beginners, say it first in their mother tongue and then in English.

'I am calm and relaxed. I observe my breathing, but I don't control it. I am calm and relaxed (pause). I can hear some noises, but they don't disturb me. I am calm and relaxed.'

2 'I can feel my feet in my shoes. I am calm and relaxed' (pause).

'I can feel my feet in my shoes. I can feel the chair under my thighs. I am calm and relaxed (pause). I can hear some noises, but they don't disturb me. I am calm and relaxed' (pause).

'I observe my breathing, but I don't control it' (pause).

'I can feel my back against the back of my chair. I am calm and relaxed' (pause).

'I can feel my arms on my desk. I am calm and relaxed. My whole body is calm and relaxed' (pause).

'I observe my breathing, but I don't control it' (pause).

'My feet are heavy, pleasantly heavy (pause). I am calm, quiet, and relaxed (pause). My feet are heavy, pleasantly heavy. I am calm, quiet, and relaxed' (longer pause).

3 Proceed similarly with all parts of the body. End by saying:

'My whole body is heavy, pleasantly heavy. I am calm, quiet, and relaxed.'

'Some parts of my body are warm, pleasantly warm, but a cool breeze is blowing on my forehead.'

Pause, repeat, and pause again.

Say, 'I am totally calm, quiet, and relaxed' (longer pause).

4 If you are satisfied that the class are relaxed, say: 'Imagine the classroom little by little and when you have a complete picture, slowly open your eyes.'

C Breathing in English

1 Ask your students to sit comfortably (see above, A) and to close their eyes.

2 In a slow, clear voice, ask them to relax as indicated in (B), but this time thinking of their shoulders, their chest, throat, neck, and diaphragm. The summary at the end should run like this:

'My chest is relaxed, my shoulders are relaxed, my throat is relaxed, my diaphragm and my chest move calmly and slowly. I am smiling.'

'I am breathing in and out, but I do not control my breathing; I observe my calm breathing.'

Pause.

3 Continue:
'I can feel the air coming in and my chest expanding. My whole body from my legs up to my throat is expanding.'

'As I slowly breathe out, I feel my throat, the upper part of my chest contracting, and gradually my whole body contracting.'

'I breathe in and out. I am calm, I am relaxed.'

Observe the class to see if they are relaxed or not. If not, repeat the instructions in (2) very slowly.

4 Say a pleasant, simple text that the learners can understand easily, for example:

'The sun is shining, my smile is shining, I am smiling in English.'

'I am breathing peacefully, there is a pleasant wind in the classroom, I am breathing in English.'

The learners articulate the text, but do not say it out loud.

5 Ask your students to open their eyes and to go on breathing like this. Ask them to do some oral pair work, still breathing calmly as they do this.

FOLLOW-UP 1

Advise your students to relax like this at home, preferably lying down comfortably to practise saying words or texts. They can listen to a recording and allow the words to permeate them.

FOLLOW-UP 2

In future lessons begin oral exercises with this activity. Very soon your students will be able to relax and breathe with their whole bodies almost instantly. In particular, encourage shy students to think of their breathing and to calmly observe the movements of their body as they breathe in and out before they start speaking.

VARIATION

For some of the activities in this book your students will need to be able to hear the language without understanding it. At the end of Step B2, suggest:

1 'I am calm, quiet, and relaxed. I can hear some noise outside but it doesn't disturb me (pause). I am going to hear a text, but I am not going to understand it. I will just enjoy hearing how it sounds (pause). I am calm, quiet, and relaxed.'

2 Play the recording of the text, gradually fading it in. (If you are saying it yourself, change your tone of voice and delivery.) In a voice that is slow, but loud enough to be heard above the recording, say:

'I am calm, quiet, and relaxed' and add, 'I can hear some pleasant sounds I don't understand (pause). The sounds resound inside me (pause for 5 seconds). I can hear pleasant, meaningless sounds (pause). I am calm, quiet, and relaxed (pause). I can hear pleasant, meaningless sounds.'

3 Draw the students' attention to the aspect you want to concentrate on (for example, rhythm, intonation, or tone of voice). Say:

'I can hear the [intonation]'

Give the learners time to take this in, then return to step B3 above, saying 'Some parts of my body are warm ...'

COMMENTS

Relaxation is essential to ensure learning takes place at a deeper level. This depth is crucial for many aspects of pronunciation and in particular to eradicate fossilized mistakes (see Chapter 4).

Acknowledgements

I learnt about these techniques through Bernard Dufeu's work at Mainz University (see Dufeu 1992, 1994). I would also like to thank Jean Auquier, psychologist and librarian, for his interesting comments.

1.2 Put on your English shoes

LEVEL

All (beginners can do the activity in their mother tongue)

TIME

10–15 minutes the first time, about 5 minutes on subsequent occasions

AIMS

Helping learners to slip into an English personality

MATERIALS

Optional: advertisements with photographs and descriptions of shoes or other clothes

PREPARATION

Make sure you know all the vocabulary that your students may require to describe shoes: types, decoration, etc. so that you can help your students out if necessary. Alternatively bring in advertisements or manufacturers' descriptions of shoes (they are pleased to send information if you write).

PROCEDURE

1 Put your students in pairs and ask them to describe the shoes they usually wear to their partners, and to say why they like them.

2 If you are teaching younger learners, just ask them to decide what shoes they feel they would like for their English classes. With adolescents and adults, you may find it useful to explain that the Chinese thinker, Confucius, once said that it is impossible to understand someone if one cannot put on their shoes. So, tell them they are going to buy a pair of new shoes, just for their English classes. Money is no object. Ask them to describe this new pair of shoes, different from the ones they are wearing. Insist that the shoes must be very comfortable and that they must be happy to wear them. Help out with any vocabulary. Alternatively, hand out the advertisements you have brought in, and ask your students to choose a pair of shoes they would like for their English classes.

3 In pairs they describe to each other what shoes they have chosen for their English classes, or they explain to each other why they have chosen the pair they have from the advertisements. They must express why they are so comfortable and so attractive.

4 Ask your students to close their eyes, to visualize their new pair of shoes, and to repeat to themselves mentally why their English shoes are so beautiful and comfortable.

5 In further lessons, start by asking your students to visualize their English shoes and to repeat to themselves why they like them. Ask them to explain quickly to another partner why they like their English shoes. Now proceed with your lesson.

VARIATION

If more appropriate—for cultural reasons or because of the situation in which you are teaching—choose another piece of clothing. If in doubt, ask your learners what piece of clothing they would associate with the language, and start from there. For British English, think of an English sweater, shirt, or blouse, English trousers, an English dress, skirt, etc. 'My English umbrella' could be an excellent choice. For American English, you might want to choose an American shirt, a hat, jeans, Bermuda shorts, a belt, boots, or a scarf.

FOLLOW-UP

You may like to progressively get your students completely dressed in English clothes. Add a piece of English clothing every time. Eventually ask your students to mentally put on their English clothes before starting the lesson.

COMMENTS

More activities aimed at improving learners' motivation and confidence can be found in *Classroom Dynamics* (Hadfield 1992), in this series.

1.3 What I can do in English

LEVEL   All (beginners may need to use their mother tongue)

TIME   10–15 minutes

AIMS   Building learner confidence

PREPARATION   Do this after the class has already had some opportunity to work together, so that they have some idea about their performance in English.

PROCEDURE   1 Ask your class to form groups of about four where they can vent their feelings easily, so allow them to choose their partners. Encourage them to talk about their worries, frustrations, and problems in their study of English, focusing on pronunciation. I often hear things like: 'I find it impossible to remember stress', 'I feel I'm a complete jerk when I try to imitate the intonation', 'I always fear they won't understand me', 'I am sure they will understand me all right, but I fear I won't understand them.' Allow this to go on for a maximum of five minutes.

2 Tell your students you have had similar fears when learning a language, but that what helped you a lot was to realize what you *could* do well.

3 Ask the class to think about and write down what they can do well in English (if they are beginners they can list words that they know they can pronounce well). They should also list two or three things they feel the other students in their group can do well, for example, 'I like the way you make yourself clearly understood', 'I wish my pronunciation was as good as yours.'

4 The learners should now write down the good things they have heard, or come to realize, about their pronunciation, and that they can accept.

5 Encourage them to keep a diary in which they monitor their progress, or to write positive comments on strips of paper that they can decorate their rooms with.

FOLLOW-UP   Do this again after some time, so that your students can recognize what progress they have made.

COMMENTS   Similar activities on grammar and vocabulary will also help your learners to break the 'sound barrier'. *Classroom Dynamics* (Hadfield 1992) contains more confidence builders; see also *The Confidence Book* (Davis and Rinvolucri 1990).

1.4 English in my life

LEVEL

All (see Variation 2 for young learners)

TIME

10–15 minutes

AIMS

Discovering what past relationship learners have had with English, dealing with prejudice about how the language sounds

MATERIALS

A class set of one of the questionnaires below

PREPARATION

Make a class set of one of the questionnaires below, or of one better adapted to your learners. For complete beginners make one in the learners' mother tongue. If you are preparing your own questionnaire, think of all the possible contacts they may have had with the language, not forgetting historical ones. Think of what they might reproach native speakers for, and what might attract them. What received opinions might there be among their family, neighbours, and friends? If you know their attitude is quite negative, try to highlight positive aspects.

1 Explain to your students—if necessary in their mother tongue—that they have probably heard English before, and may associate it with personal experiences. Give some examples of your own if you are not a native speaker, or give examples of what you have heard or noticed, trying to give positive and negative ones. Examples (for British English):

'My first experience of English was listening to the BBC World Service. I would fiddle with the controls of the short-wave radio when my parents were away from home. I was fascinated by the Morse signal for 'V' which started the broadcasts, followed by a bass voice saying "This is London". I can still hear the voice ringing in my ears.

I associated this with the liberation of my country at the end of the Second World War.'

'On the other hand I have heard that Americans say the British speak with a plum in their mouth.'

2 Tell them you are going to hand out a questionnaire to fill in, which they will discuss later. It is about their contacts with English in the past. Make it clear there are no 'right' or 'wrong' answers. Do not give them too much time to fill this in. Their answers should be as spontaneous as possible. Provide help if needed, but do not hover over the students to monitor—they need to be alone with themselves.

The sample questionnaire includes a complete range of views, but you can adapt it to your class. For example, if you know your students have a very negative view of English, highlight the positive aspects. Students can also help compose the questionnaire themselves; this brings their attitudes into the open.

1 _____ (relatives or friends) can speak English.

2 _____ (relatives or friends) do not like the way English sounds because
_____.

3 I hear English in my daily life when _____
_____
at (place) _____
I like/don't like it because _____
_____.

4 _____ are people I know who speak English and I don't like them
because _____
_____.

5 _____ are people I know who speak English and I like them because
_____
_____.

6 I think English sounds nice because _____
_____.

7 I don't think English sounds nice because _____
_____.

8 In the past my country had bad/good experiences with English-speaking countries
when _____
_____.

9 At present the relationship between my country and the governments of English-
speaking countries is _____
because _____
_____.

10 I expect English will be easy to pronounce for me because _____
_____
_____.

11 I expect English will not be very easy for me to pronounce because _____
_____
_____.

12 When I speak English I want people to believe I am British/American because
_____
_____.

13 When I speak English I hope people will not think I am British/American because
_____
_____.

14 When I speak English I think people will not believe I am British/American because
_____
_____.

15 I like the English language, but I am not sure I would like to live in England (or
America, Australia, Canada, Ireland, New Zealand, etc.) because _____
_____
_____.

3 Ask your students to discuss the points raised in pairs and to change pairs a couple of times.

VARIATION 1

1 Prepare a 'Find someone who' questionnaire like the one below (see Moskowitz 1978: 50–2), and hand it out.

2 Tell your students they only have a limited time to ask as many people as possible the questions and briefly discuss their reasons for answering the way they did. You may find it best not to monitor, but just to be available in case they need linguistic help. Afterwards allow the class to volunteer any comments they wish to the whole group, but without mentioning any names.

SAMPLE QUESTIONNAIRE

Find someone ...

1 who has a relative who speaks English well.

2 who would like to speak like a native speaker.

3 who would not like to be confused with a native speaker.

4 who likes English spoken with an Australian accent.

5 whose country was freed by British/American/Canadian/ Australian soldiers.

6 who thinks English is very easy to pronounce.

7 who fears English may be difficult to pronounce.

8 who likes hearing English spoken with a BBC accent.

9 who does not like English pop songs.

10 who finds English is a very musical language.

11 who finds it amusing to make pronunciation mistakes in English.

12 whose parents hate the way English sounds.

13 who has dreamt in English.

14 who likes the English language but would not like to live in Britain/America/Australia, etc.

15 whose country was a British/American colony in the past.

16 who hopes people will guess what his or her mother tongue is when he or she speaks English.

17 who is afraid some people will laugh when he or she speaks English.

18 who is satisfied with the way he or she speaks English.

VARIATION 2

For younger learners:

Ask them to make a drawing of what they associate English with.

'English in my life' by Charles, age 6: going on holiday with a
caravan. The original is orange and red.

COMMENTS   Students can make up questionnaires like these themselves—it is
stimulating and brings other attitudes towards language out into
the open.

1.5 My perception of English

LEVEL   All except young learners

TIME   15–20 minutes

AIMS   Making students aware of how they perceive English,
helping them to overcome their prejudices

MATERIALS   A class set of one of the questionnaires below or of a
similar questionnaire

PREPARATION   Prepare a class set of one of the questionnaires below, or make
up a similar questionnaire, better adapted to your students. If

you adapt it, think of the circumstances in which your students are likely to have come into contact with English. Begin with apparently innocuous questions and move on to more probing ones. Ask questions that involve all the senses. For beginners do this in their mother tongue.

PROCEDURE

1 Explain to your students that they are going to explore how they react to the sound of English. They will work in pairs and change pairs twice. Allow the students to choose their partners each time. Hand out the questionnaires.

2 The students read the questionnaire and decide how they feel about the choice proposed, and also what they think their partner feels about English. They should choose quickly, without thinking too much. The partners should tell each other how they think the other relates to English. Then they discuss what they have said.

3 With the whole class, ask students to say what they have discovered and anything that they have found striking.

SAMPLE QUESTIONNAIRES

Questionnaire 1

When you hear English:

1 a it is like the sound of waves breaking on the beach
   b it is like the sound of a mountain brook

2 a it brings back memories of winter[1]
   b it brings back memories of summer

3 a it makes you feel like dancing
   b it makes you feel like sleeping

4 a it reminds you of eating an apple[2]
   b it reminds you of eating a banana

5 a you can smell flowers
   b you can smell food

6 a it sounds ideal for giving orders
   b it sounds ideal for courtship

Photocopiable © Oxford University Press

Notes

1 Or it reminds you of the rainy season/the dry season, where this is more appropriate.

2 Or two kinds of fruit with contrasting textures which are common where you work.

Questionnaire 2

When you hear English:

1 **a** you associate it with a radiator
   b you associate it with a fridge

2 **a** it reminds you of an orange
   b it reminds you of a lemon

4 **a** it smells like a meadow
   b it smells like a town

5 **a** it reminds you of your father
   b it reminds you of your mother

6 **a** it sounds more like German[1]
   b it sounds more like French

Photocopiable © Oxford University Press

Note

1 Or two languages your students hear occasionally, or study.

Questionnaire 3

When you hear English:

1 **a** you associate it with the sun
   b you associate it with the moon

2 **a** it reminds you of fish
   b it reminds you of roast beef

3 **a** it sounds like a violin[1]
   b it sounds like a drum

4 **a** you feel like running
   b you feel like strolling

5 **a** you think of a brother/an uncle/a male cousin
   b you think of a sister/an aunt/a female cousin

6 **a** you feel it is ideal for singing in
   b you feel it is ideal for shouting in

Photocopiable © Oxford University Press

Note

1 Or two contrasting instruments your students are familiar with.

VARIATION 1

Prepare a questionnaire with four choices: a, b, c, and d, and pin or stick a sign with one of these on in each corner of your classroom. For each question, all the students who choose 'a' go to corner 'a', etc. Give the people in each corner a few minutes to discuss their choice, then go on to the next question. They should not spend too long choosing.

SAMPLE QUESTIONNAIRE

When you hear English:

1 a you think of a tunnel
   b you think of a bridge
   c you think of a hot-air balloon
   d you think of a raft

2 a you can taste bread
   b you can taste chocolate
   c you can taste salt
   d you can taste sand

3 a you hear a cat purring
   b you hear the rain on a window
   c you hear footsteps in the snow
   d you hear the siren of an ambulance

4 a you feel excited
   b you feel worried
   c you feel light-headed
   d you feel tired

5 a you think of the Queen of England[1]
   b you think of Keanu Reeves
   c you think of Kim Basinger
   d you think of the President of the United States

Photocopiable © Oxford University Press

Note

1 Choose figures your learners are likely to know, for example politicians, pop or film stars, or sports people.

VARIATION 2

Ask your students to associate the sound of English with things they can touch and see in class, or the voices of people they can hear in school or at work. Do not forget the food served at school or at work! Ask them to actually look at the objects and touch them whenever possible.

Examples

Touch a rough wall, a wooden door, the window pane, tissue paper, a leather school bag, a piece of chalk

Sight the blackboard, a tree outside, the floor, a goldfish in a bowl, the sports hall

Taste last week's lunches

Voices the principal/boss, the school nurse/secretary, the caretaker, the maths teacher, the telephone operator

COMMENTS

This kind of activity can be repeated at intervals, using different questionnaires. Get your students to help write the questions.

1.6 Listen to the sound of English

'Listening is an action.' (Auriol 1991: 15)

LEVEL

All

TIME

15 minutes +

AIMS

Approaching the sound of the language in terms of its affective value and its aesthetic impact, discovering why learners may not like the language, and finding reasons to like it by listening and looking at it anew

MATERIALS

Recordings spoken by different native speakers whose voices and ways of speaking you like

PREPARATION

Prepare recordings as described in Materials. It is not necessary for the learners to actually understand what the speakers say. My personal choice would include: John Gielgud, Joan Collins, George Alagiah and Kate Adie (BBC reporters), Joan Baez, and Michael York. Use your local variety of English if more appropriate. You could use tapes from your coursebook.

PROCEDURE

1 Tell your students you are going to play recordings of people speaking English, and that you would like them to give their impressions about how it sounds.

2 Play the recordings, twice if necessary. Put your students into groups of up to four, and ask them to express how the language sounds to them. Suggest they begin their sentences with 'English is ...' or 'English sounds ...'

Some examples of what learners say:

Age 13: 'English sounds romantic, ... strange.'
'It is fast, ... more expressive than French, ... quiet and sweet, ... more musical than Dutch.'

Age 14: 'English sounds musical, ... zany, ... fulfilling, ... aggressive, ... less expressive than German, ... less pleasant than Dutch.'

Age 20: 'English is sensuous and sexy, ... musical, ... dignified.'

Some learners' preference for one variety of English may also come up, for example:

Age 19: 'British English sounds like American English.'
'Americans don't articulate at all.'

'British English is purer than American English.'
'American English is too fast.'

3 Do this again in different groups.

4 Let them discuss their ideas as a class, allowing them to express any views they like. If they do not like any of the voices, encourage them to say if they have ever heard any other speakers they do like.

FOLLOW-UP

Encourage your learners to bring in recordings they like of people speaking English and to say why they like them. They could also do this for voices they do not like.

VARIATION 1

Ask your learners to make a list of five languages and rank them in order, beginning with the one they find the most beautiful. They should include English. They discuss their choices in pairs first, and with the whole class later.

VARIATION 2

Ask your students to compare the way English sounds with other languages. Their subjective general impressions are sufficient, but you could bring in some recorded samples of other languages (or ask your students to find samples), for example excerpts from news bulletins.

VARIATION 3

1 With the help of your class, make a list of people they hear speaking English (film, radio, television).

2 Ask them to rank them in order of preference based on the way they speak.

3 They discuss their preferences, first in pairs, and then as a class.

VARIATION 4

1 Instead of sound recordings, use videos of speakers your students could identify with or could look up to. Using the sound without the pictures, follow the main procedure.

2 Show the pictures with the sound. The students decide if they still like the same people.

3 In pairs, the students imitate the speaker they like most: posture, attitude, and voice. The other student tries to guess who they are imitating and the pairs discuss the reasons why the imitator likes the chosen person.

VARIATION 5

Young learners, especially if they cannot write English yet, can do this activity by drawing what they feel English sounds like. The example overleaf is by Léa, age 6.

1.7 Which face is English?

LEVEL All except very young learners

TIME 10 minutes

AIMS Becoming aware of the facial expressions of native speakers

MATERIALS Magazine pictures; video recordings for the Variation

PREPARATION Find photographs (cut out from magazines, for example) of people speaking different languages, including English. Include a second-generation speaker from the immigrant community (Asian, Jamaican, etc.). The clothes should not be a give-away.

PROCEDURE

1 Ask your students if they can recognize native English speakers by the expression on their face, even when they cannot hear them talk. Ask them if they can recognize the mother tongue of people in general, simply by the kind of face they make.

2 In groups, the students make 'English' faces to each other and discuss them. Ask one person from each group to report to the whole class. Do not betray agreement or disagreement with any of the ideas presented.

3 Show the students pictures of people speaking different languages (including English). In their groups they try to recognize who is speaking English, and discuss how they recognize them.

4 The group representatives report back to the class. Give the students the right answer and allow them to react.

VARIATION

1 This works better with video. You need about five one-minute video recordings of people speaking a variety of languages, of which two at least should be speaking English. If any of the English-speaking people pronounces a 'th', make sure you also have a speaker of a language where a similar sound is pronounced, for example Spanish.

2 First play the video with the sound off. After the students have made their guesses, play it with the sound on.

FOLLOW-UP

Encourage your students to collect pictures or put together a video recording to be used in a later lesson. Do not use it immediately; wait a couple of weeks to give your students' subconscious awareness an opportunity to evolve before they try again.

COMMENTS

This will help learners to become aware of the stereotypes they have, and help them to accept that they can speak English in one of its varieties and still have a face that is acceptable to themselves. Progressively they will realize that the body language, the clothes, the situation, or the background in the video or the pictures may be the real points that have helped them.

1.8 Play back

LEVEL

All

TIME

5–10 minutes

AIMS

Preparing learners to speak by helping them look like native speakers, without actually speaking

MATERIALS

An audio or video tape of people speaking, singing, or acting in English, a class set of transcripts

PREPARATION

Choose recordings to suit the level and interests of your students: for example, extracts from the news or TV series aimed at younger people, raps, songs, or poems. A video is best for the first few times you do this. Transcribe the text and make copies.

PROCEDURE

1 Play the video once to the learners. Tell them they are going to 'play it back', i.e. act as if they were singing or speaking but without actually doing so. Demonstrate by playing the video or audio tape and mouthing the words. Make appropriate gestures as well.

2 Hand out the transcript to the students and ask them all to 'play back', while you play the tape. Do the same yourself.

3 Use the sound track only (turn the TV round, for instance), and ask the class to 'play back' again.

4 Ask for a volunteer to 'play back' in front of the class, while the others do it from their seats.

5 Ask if anyone is now ready to 'play back' alone or in groups, actually speaking/singing this time. It is important that you use volunteers only.

FOLLOW-UP

Choose a good student to take the place of the video or tape, while the other students 'play back'. Activity 1.9 takes this one important step further.

COMMENTS

1 With teenagers it is better to begin with songs, then go on with spoken texts.

2 If you cannot use video, ask students to think of a passage in a film they have seen at the cinema and replay that.

1.9 Make an English face

LEVEL

All

TIME

5–10 minutes

AIMS

Encouraging your students to use their face muscles in the ways native speakers do to find appropriate articulatory settings

MATERIALS

A video tape of people speaking English, or extracts from commercially-produced ELT videos

PREPARATION

1 Students do activity 1.8 a couple of times before doing this one.

2 Select several two-minute video recordings of people (speaking English) that your students can identify with.

PROCEDURE

1 Ask your students to describe what they think an English-speaking face looks like, and to demonstrate in a relaxed

atmosphere. In countries where films are dubbed in the local language, discuss the effect that results from the facial expressions not fitting the language that comes out of the mouths of the actors.

2 Arrange the class in groups of three. One student can see the TV screen, the back of the second is turned towards the set, and the third can observe the other two.

3 Explain that the students facing the screen will have to imitate the facial movements of the person speaking on the video. Those with their backs towards the screen imitate those who can see. The observers will provide feedback.

4 Proceed as described in Step 3. The learners discuss their performance and how they feel about it.

FOLLOW-UP

If you have access to a video camera, you can plug the camera into the television set and get the students to speak to themselves in English, and observe their own facial movements.

VARIATION

If you cannot use video, ask your learners to think of characters in films they have seen. They work in pairs and one of them imitates while the other gives feedback. Encourage them to observe characters in films after the initial activity and to come and imitate a character in class later. The class exchange their ideas.

1.10 The ventriloquist

LEVEL

All

TIME

5–10 minutes

AIMS

Encouraging your students to use their faces like native speakers do

MATERIALS

A number of dolls or puppets if possible

PROCEDURE

1 Tell your students they are going to play at being ventriloquists. Explain that British speakers are famous for not moving their mouths very much when they speak and that this is very much like being a 'ventriloquist'. Discuss how ventriloquists work.

2 Demonstrate yourself with a doll, puppet, or something symbolizing a doll (a ruler, for example). You need not be brilliant at this. Concentrate on trying to keep your upper lip still and moving the rest of your face as little as possible. If you are not too good, this will make it easier for your shy learners to try!

3 Pair your students off. One is a ventriloquist, the other observes and provides feedback. They either improvise a dialogue or practise one they have studied in class, if that makes them more comfortable. Then they swap roles.

FOLLOW-UP 1

Encourage your students to practise this at home, possibly in front of a mirror, and allow them to come and demonstrate their ability to be a ventriloquist whenever they like. Encourage them to have spontaneous dialogues in class, acting as ventriloquists.

FOLLOW-UP 2

Encourage students to use a classmate as a 'doll'. One of them pretends to speak—but does not—and the other one speaks.

COMMENTS

This activity greatly helps students whose mother tongue requires a lot of facial movement to find articulatory settings that suit English. It is especially suitable for British English.

1.11 Finding my English/American voice

'The roots of voice come from deep inside the individual.'
(Estienne 1993: 15)

LEVEL

All

TIME

5–10 minutes

AIMS

Helping your students to use their speech organs like native speakers do, especially Americans

PROCEDURE

1 Ask your learners to stand against a wall, with the whole of the spine touching the wall and their backs absolutely straight—there should be no hollow anywhere. Their feet should be about a foot apart, their knees very slightly bent, and their chins very slightly lowered (not pointing upwards).

2 Ask them to say a sentence in their mother tongue, preferably with their eyes closed, and to listen to the depth and power of their voice.

3 Ask them to say it again with their chins raised. They should notice that their voice is less powerful and less rich. Point out that it is important not to raise one's chin as it affects voice quality.

4 Get your students to breathe as described in 1.1C and to relax their speech organs: upper lip, tongue, larynx (see 1.1B).

5 When you can see they are quiet and relaxed, ask them to listen as you say the following (or a similar text):

'I am going to hear my American voice.

My American voice is calm and relaxed.

'I say "no"; I am relaxed.

I say "why?"; I am relaxed.

I say "how".'

Then say some more, slightly longer utterances, at their level. For example, at elementary level you can say things like:

'I say "evening".

I say "good evening".

I say "I'm all right".'

6 If you are satisfied with the way this is going, say 'This is my American voice. I like my American voice.'

7 Do an oral activity—a very short one at first—asking your students to feel the same relaxation as before.

FOLLOW-UP   Do this every now and again before your students do an oral activity. Encourage them to prepare themselves in this way at home before practising.

COMMENTS   As the introductory quotation says, our voice is an essential part of our identity. Sounding foreign to oneself is an important and potentially difficult experience. The activity helps to overcome this as well as to find proper articulatory settings for English.

Acknowledgements

The description of the position comes from Estienne 1993.

1.12 Imitate native speakers

'How come you suddenly pronounce English so well?'

'I am making fun of them when they speak our language.'

(Jonathan, age 11)

LEVEL   **All**

TIME   **20 minutes the first time, about 10 minutes on subsequent occasions**

AIMS   **Helping to overcome fears of sounding 'ridiculous' and providing a mental model for learners to aim at**

MATERIALS   **Texts in your learners' mother tongue and in English. For Variation 1: a recording, possibly a video, of English speakers speaking the learners' language with a strong accent**

PREPARATION

Choose or write two dialogues at an appropriate level for your students to act out, one in their mother tongue, the other in English. If your students have different mother tongues, try Variation 2.

PROCEDURE

1 Ask your class if they have ever heard British/American people speak the students' language. Ask them to describe how they sound and how one can recognize them by the way they speak. Do not be offended if they make fun of British/American people.

2 Hand out the text in your students' mother tongue. In pairs, they try to imitate British or American people as they say the dialogue.

3 The pairs discuss who imitated the British or Americans most convincingly, and why. Praise the best imitators, and encourage them to play to the whole class.

4 Ask the students to sit comfortably and to close their eyes. In a quiet, soft, and persuasive voice, tell them to say anything they like to themselves with an English/American accent, and to listen with their inner ear.

5 Point out that if your learners speak English with the accents British or American people have when they speak your learners' mother tongue, they will speak English more like British or American people. Tell them they are going to try this.

6 Hand out the text of the dialogue in English. The students say it in pairs, still imitating British or American people. They change partners. Monitor, moving from pair to pair, and make sure you praise some aspect of their performance.

VARIATION 1

1 Bring in an audio or video recording of native speakers speaking your students' language with a strong English/American accent. In some countries films with Oliver Hardy and Stan Laurel, intentionally dubbed with a strong accent, do the trick very well. (Make sure you act in accordance with performance rights regulations as applicable in your country.) Choose a characteristic passage that can be imitated by your students (level, content). Prepare a script of the dialogue, and another in English.

2 Play the audio or video tape twice. The second time, encourage the learners to imitate the speakers quietly to themselves whenever they find them particularly 'amusing'.

3 Ask the students to say at what moments they found the pronunciation particularly funny, and encourage them to imitate the speakers. Ask if anyone can explain why they think the British/Americans pronounce the students' language in that way.

4 Hand out the text of the dialogue and encourage students, in pairs, to act out the passage from the film or tape, imitating the

speakers in any way possible. The class can make any comments they like.

5 Hand out another short dialogue in English and ask the class to act it out, still imagining they are the speakers they heard on the tape or in the film.

VARIATION 2

1 If your students have different native languages, put them in groups or pairs according to language and ask them to discuss what British/American people sound like when they speak the students' languages.

2 Ask each group to prepare a short dialogue in their native language. Ask them to act it out, imitating the way British/American people speak.

3 The groups discuss their performance and try to make it still more British/American.

4 Hand out the English dialogues you have prepared and ask your students to play them, still mentally imitating British/American people speaking a foreign language.

FOLLOW-UP 1

Ask your students to try to listen to native English speakers speaking your students' mother tongue, and to report whenever they notice something new. If possible, ask them to make recordings and to bring them into class to be used as explained above.

FOLLOW-UP 2

More advanced learners can try to imitate speakers of other languages when they speak English.

FOLLOW-UP 3

In future lessons, encourage the students to think about how the British/Americans pronounce the students' language(s). For this ask them to relax (see 1.1B), close their eyes, and imagine British/American people speaking the students' language(s). It will take one minute at the most, but can have a very beneficial effect.

1.13 Transmit your feeling of English

LEVEL

Post-beginners and above

TIME

5–10 minutes, plus preparation time

AIMS

Giving students an opportunity to feel how others feel English through their bodies

MATERIALS

A short rhyme or poem adapted to your students' age, level, and interests

PREPARATION

Teach your students part of a popular song (the chorus for example), a nursery rhyme, or a poem that appeals to them. They need to know it by heart. At first it is better to have the same poem or rhyme for all the students, but later you can use different ones, possibly written by the students (see 2.11). Ask your students to practise it at home, relaxing and breathing as explained in 1.1.

PROCEDURE

1 Next lesson, tell your students that they are going to communicate how they feel English in their bodies to a partner. Allow them to choose their partners for this. Ideally they should sit comfortably on the floor, otherwise on chairs, one behind the other. The ones in front close their eyes, while the ones behind observe their partners.

2 Get your students to relax, breathe slowly and deeply (see 1.1B and C), and synchronize their breathing with their partners. When this is achieved, ask the students in front to say the rhyme or poem quietly, still breathing in time with their partners, but also following the feeling the poem gives them.

3 The pairs reverse roles and repeat the activity, then discuss their feelings about it.

VARIATION

1 If it is culturally acceptable to your students, or if you can progressively build up group cohesion and trust to the point where students can touch each other, ask them to sit as in Step 1 above. The ones who are sitting behind put both hands on their partner's back.

2 They close their eyes, relax as directed by you, and follow the breathing directly through this contact while the students in front say the poem/rhyme.

FOLLOW-UP

Ask each student to select and prepare a short rhyme or poem and teach it to their partner. Then proceed as above.

COMMENTS

1 See Further Reading for some sources of suitable poems and rhymes.

2 Though I personally prefer to use texts which aim to be beautiful, you can teach the inherent beauty of everyday utterances as well.

3 People's relationship to a language often hinges on their aesthetic perception of that language. This activity helps students to communicate their sense of beauty to each other, greatly improves the group dynamic, and gives a feeling of the rhythm of the language.

Acknowledgements

This is adapted from an activity I learnt from Joan Agosta.

2 The beat and tune of English

It is impossible to speak without rhythm and intonation, and these 'suprasegmentals' deeply affect the quality of speech sounds (phonemes).

But these aspects have often been presented as the 'unteachables' of pronunciation. Rhythm and intonation are focal points of personal resistance to learning. But 'unteachable' does not necessarily mean 'unlearnable'.

This resistance is probably due to the fact that the rhythm and intonation of our mother tongue are very intimately linked with our identity. They are possibly the first external noises the unborn baby hears (Tomatis 1977), and they are also the first elements of the language that babies reproduce (see, for example, Crystal 1986). This in itself can justify the importance of learning these first, but research also points to a high correlation between the ability to feel, perceive, and analyse pace and rhythm and learning abilities in general, in particular the ability to learn a language (Alahuhta 1980 and 1986, cited in Auriol 1991: 105–6).

Because of all the points above, we could claim that by starting with suprasegmentals we are following a 'natural' as well as a logical and pedagogical order.

How can we teach stress and intonation?

There are many aspects involved in stress and intonation. An incomplete list would include stress, rhythm, rate of delivery, pausing, loudness, pitch, voice quality, the speaker's intentions, attitude, mood, etc., all combined with context, grammar, and discourse. Because of the variety and the complexity of the factors, the approach in this book is in essence non-analytical.

The first activities in this chapter aim at arousing a sense of rhythm in general. Then rhythm is associated with stress and language, and a variety of activities gradually approach utterances in terms of rhythm, tune, voice quality, body language, sensory perception, affective response, and aesthetic sense.

As rhythm and intonation are tied to context, learners are then helped to associate meaning/context and intonation contours: stress/rhythm and intonation are separated here purely for reasons of clarity.

The most effective approach is to alternate activities from this chapter with activities for improving individual speech sounds (see Chapter 3) and tackling personal resistance (see Chapter 1). All of these should be woven in as you observe your learners' development.

Some follow-ups and activities are nearer to more conventional practice to show how to gradually help more analytical learners. These activities help to complete and refine the framework. When the foundations have been built, and learners have allowed rhythm and intonation to take shape within them, then they can usefully build more consciously on these foundations.

2.1 Walking the rhythm

LEVEL	**All (in the mother tongue at beginner and elementary level)**
TIME	**10–15 minutes**
AIMS	**Developing awareness of pace and rhythm**
MATERIALS	**Music to accompany walking and rhythmic texts, recorded if possible (see Preparation)**

PREPARATION

1 Select a piece of music to walk to, for example, 'Promenade' from Mussorgsky's *Pictures at an Exhibition* (piano version), or Elgar's *Pomp and Circumstance March* no 1, 'Land of hope and glory'.

2 Also make a recording, if possible, of a short poem or prose text in English and one in your students' language. At elementary level a rhyme such as 'Thirty days has September' (see page 51) is very suitable. Wordsworth's 'Daffodils' is very appropriate at more advanced levels. A recording of Sir John Betjeman reading one of his poems would also be suitable. It is a good idea to try the activity yourself first.

PROCEDURE

1 Ask the learners to walk round the room in pairs, with one leading, and the other trying to walk like the leader. The leaders should move as they like—stop, slow down, or speed up. After a maximum of one minute, ask the students to swap roles. After another minute, ask all the students to stop and discuss the way they felt, first in groups of four, then as a class. Provide any linguistic help that may be needed.

2 Play the music and ask the students to walk to it. Then ask

how easy or natural it is for them to walk to the pace of the music.

3 Play the recording of a short poem, or read it and encourage your students to move a part of their body (for example, head, leg, or arm) or to sway their whole body to the rhythm of the text.

4 Next, play the recording (or read the poem) again and ask your students to walk to the rhythm of the text. Then they comment on how it felt to walk to the rhythm of the English text.

5 Repeat Step 4, but your students should go on walking to the rhythm after the poem has finished. They are now feeling the rhythm of English inside themselves.

6 In monolingual classes, proceed as in Step 4 with a poem or prose text in your students' mother tongue. Then allow them to express any differences they feel there are between the rhythm of English and that of their native language. Stress that there are no 'right' or 'wrong' impressions.

FOLLOW-UP

1 Encourage your students to read the poem aloud at home, walking to the pace of the stresses on the words, or shaking their heads or moving any part of their body to the rhythm. Ideally they should listen to a recording to guide them—if they do not have one, make sure they know where the stress falls.

2 Whether your students are beginners or more advanced learners, it is essential to build on this and develop a feeling for rhythm—see the other activities in this chapter. You should also start developing a feeling for the tune or intonation of English in parallel (see 2.17 and the following activities).

VARIATION

If there is not enough space in your classroom for the whole class to walk around, either work with small groups in turn, or ask the students to clap, nod, or move an arm or a leg instead of walking.

2.2 Slow down!

LEVEL

All except very young learners

TIME

10–15 minutes the first time, a couple of minutes in subsequent lessons

AIMS

Doing away with pressure to speak quickly in English

MATERIALS

A 2–3 minute recording of quiet, slow music that is acceptable (age/culture) to your students, and class copies of a short text

PREPARATION

Select a suitable piece of music (see the suggestions at the end of the activity) and a short text which goes with it.

PROCEDURE

1 Ask the learners to compare the speed at which English is spoken with the speed of other languages they have heard (including their mother tongue). Do not comment. They can do this in groups and then report back to the whole class.

2 The learners make a list of people who they feel speak quickly in their native language, some who speak slowly, and some who speak at average speed. Tell them that as some 'normal', proficient native speakers speak English *twice as slowly* as others, there is no need for learners to speak quickly.

3 Explain that from now on you would like them to speak slowly. Tell them that you are going to play some slow music, and that you would like them to speak slowly and calmly, like the music. Make it clear that speaking slowly means taking more time to speak and making vowel sounds longer, not leaving gaps between words.

4 Ask the class to sit comfortably (see 1.1A), close their eyes, and breathe slowly, allowing the music to guide their breathing. Play the music and say the short text, and ask the class to repeat it inwardly, following the pace of the music. They can move their lips but not actually speak out loud.

5 Hand out the text or put it up on the board. Ask your students to say the text to each other in pairs, still following the slow pace of the music.

6 Ask the class how it feels to speak so slowly. Invite some students to say the text in front of the class and encourage the class to clap or otherwise 'reward' the slowest students.

FOLLOW-UP

Encourage your students to choose a text and practise it with a partner. They should also practise reading or speaking slowly at home, using the same technique, with their own choice of slow music.

COMMENTS

1 This activity helps learners to find a speaking pace that suits their personality as well as English.

2 Beginners always find a new language fast because they cannot yet pick out what is really relevant in the flow of sounds, and so they try to process nearly all of them. That is why they feel compelled to speak English very quickly. They impose a rhythm that is alien to English, which makes them difficult to understand.

3 A recent study (Cabrera Abreu and Maidment 1993) shows that slow English is spoken at a speed of 3.63 syllables per second, 'normal' English at 4.72, and fast English at 5.68 syllables a second. The figures for Spanish in the same study are 5.18, 6.45, and 8.00 respectively. The important point is the difference between the fast and the slow speakers in each

language. Activity 2.13, 'With the speed of summer lightning', also deals with rate of delivery.

Suggestions for music

- Vangelis: Sound track from *La Fête sauvage* (*Wildlife Celebration*) for example, the flute solo
- New Age music: any soothing, atmospheric music
- Mozart: an excerpt from the Andantino from the Flute and Harp Concerto in C major, K 299
- Handel: Oboe and Strings Concerto no. 3 in G minor (Sarabande, Largo).

2.3 Surprise, surprise!

LEVEL

Elementary and above

TIME

10 minutes

AIMS

Getting learners to put prominence at the end of sentences

PROCEDURE

1 Explain to your class that as a general rule, when British/American people speak, they tend to slow down towards the end of a sentence because sentences tend to begin with what the listener already knows, and slow down when the new point is coming nearer. This is all the more true when the new information is very important, or has strong emotional value.

2 Ask your students to think of some really surprising news or information and to tell this to a number of other learners, speaking naturally, but, as they want to prolong the suspense, slowing down. Ask them to begin by saying something like 'I've got something surprising to tell you', 'You'll never guess what I'm going to tell you', 'Sit down, I've got some news for you'. Their partners provide feedback on how well they surprised them.

VARIATION 1

As in Procedure, but this time the learners choose a piece of important news, slowing down to make sure their partner understands well. Suggest that they act as if they were in a dramatic situation, where they have little time—for example, any kind of emergency: plotters, spies, fugitives, etc. Ask the class to begin with 'I am going to say this very slowly and I am going to say it only once' or 'I am going to tell you something really important'. The feedback is crucial.

VARIATION 2

As in Procedure again, but this time ask your students to find a fact they are angry about. They begin with 'Listen carefully, I don't want to have to repeat this'. Again, feedback is essential.

FOLLOW-UP

Use this technique to practise combining pausing, sentence stress, and intonation (rising for surprising information, rise-fall for important information) to indicate prominence. See also 2.10, 'Sentence stress'.

2.4 Pause!

LEVEL

Elementary and above

TIME

5–10 minutes the first time, a couple of minutes in later lessons

AIMS

Dealing with pressure to speak without stopping; improving communication by pausing

MATERIALS

Recordings of texts with pauses in them, and a song with a pause (optional); list of topics for discussion

PREPARATION

1 Select texts with pauses in them; choose conversations and monologues. Try to find a text recorded without pauses and one with pauses.

2 (Optional) Choose a song with a pause or pauses in it, for example, 'Heart' (My heart starts missing a beat) by the Pet Shop Boys, or ask your learners to find one for you.

3 Make a sheet with a list of topics for discussion (see below). Make a copy for each group.

PROCEDURE

1 In groups of four to six, give your learners five minutes to discuss what effect 'silence' has on speaking. They report back to the whole class afterwards.

2 Play your recording(s) and instruct the class to listen to the moments when the person *does not* speak, and to find what effect the pauses have on communication. Do this with a song if you have one too. Ask the class to list the possible meanings of silences. They should find some of the following:

- to separate groups of words that belong together (phrases or tone groups)
- to avoid ambiguity
- to signal that another idea is coming
- to think about what their partner has just said
- they do not know what to say any more

- they want to draw attention to a particular point
- the speaker has finished a sentence
- to signal a change in topic
- they are waiting for an answer or for feedback
- they want to make sure their audience is listening
- they want to give their audience time to think
- if it is really long, the speaker has finished.

3 Ask your students to pinpoint in what cases silence actually improves communication.

4 In pairs, learners practise pausing meaningfully. They can use the conclusions they found in Step 2 above, for example:

- In groups of up to four, they choose a topic from the prepared list. One of the four talks about the topic. When they want to hear the opinion of the others, the speakers stop with a questioning look. The other group members provide feedback.

- Ask your students to pause to give a surprising twist to what was said before the pause. For example:

    They do trust him—a little.
    He does not drink whisky—before seven in the morning.

- In pairs, learners take it in turns to speak, pausing slightly after each sentence. The other partner should report on the appropriateness of the pauses.

- Students prepare a short talk only thirty seconds long, which they deliver, pausing before the culminating point. Their partners provide feedback.

- Students prepare a short talk of one minute at most, divided into three parts. They must begin with a pause, and pause adequately before beginning each new part.

- Students prepare a short speech (one minute) that includes rhetorical questions for the listeners. Every time there is a rhetorical question, the speaker pauses to give the listeners time to answer mentally. After the speech, the speaker asks the listeners if they had enough time to answer the rhetorical questions and asks if their answers were the same as they expected.

- Students deliver a speech to two groups in succession. The first time they try not to stop, but the second time they build in pauses using any of the approaches above. The listeners provide feedback.

FOLLOW-UP

Discuss with your students what they can do when they are lost for words. The following list is not exhaustive:

- slow down to give themselves more time to think
- think beforehand of what they are going to speak about
- make a summary of what they have said before, so gaining time to think

- using 'fillers', also called 'lubricants', such as: 'As I have said before', 'To sum up'
- ask a rhetorical question, and give time for listeners to answer mentally: 'I wonder if you see what I mean?', 'Am I making myself clear?', 'Are you following me?'

Give your learners plenty of opportunity to speak and practise this in the following weeks.

COMMENTS

A balance has to be achieved between making liaisons between words and pausing when this leads to better understanding. The two are often linked: students stop between words or at wrong places because they do not know the right places, or these 'feel wrong' to them. For students who are too slow, see 'With the speed of summer lightning' (2.13).

2.5 Word stress

LEVEL

All

TIME

About 5 minutes

AIMS

Developing personal and physical awareness of word stress

MATERIALS

For the Variation: recordings of pieces of music with different rhythms

PREPARATION

Prepare a list of words with the same stress pattern, including nonsense words.

PROCEDURE

1 Brainstorm a number of rhythmic feelings with the class first. Make a list of fields where rhythmic activities occur (for example, music, dance, nature, sports, transport, cooking). Here are some examples of what may come out of the brainstorming:

Nature: a summer breeze, an autumn gale, the waves of the sea, breathing, heartbeats

Sports: riding a horse, rowing a boat, cycling, running, swimming, tennis

Transport: travelling by train, cars driving on a road covered with slabs of concrete.

2 Ask the learners to sit comfortably, close their eyes, and breathe calmly (see 1.1C). Tell them in a quiet voice that you are going to say some words. They should concentrate on the rhythm of the words, not the meaning, and try to associate it

with something personal, maybe from the list made in Step 1. Ask them to complete the second part of a sentence such as 'When I feel the rhythm of those words it is as if ...' or 'The rhythm of these words makes me think of ...'.

3 Quietly say the words you have prepared without stopping between them. Repeat the list.

4 Ask the learners to inwardly visualize the classroom, and when they can 'see' it, to open their eyes and tell their neighbours what they associate the stress pattern of the words with.

5 With the help of the class, write more words with the same rhythmic pattern on the board. Encourage the learners to keep a personal list of words with the same stress pattern and to write down what they associate it with.

6 The students mingle freely and find out if anyone else has made the same association as themselves. If so, put students with similar feelings into groups.

7 Ask the learners to imagine the rhythmic feeling they personally associate the stress pattern with. At a given signal, they say the words, thinking of their personal associations.

8 **(Optional)** You can also encourage the learners to move to the rhythm, or to draw (in any colour they like) their feeling of the stress pattern.

FOLLOW-UP 1

1 If your students' names can be 'anglicized' do so, or ask them to choose an English name for themselves. Get them to find the rhythm of their name and clap its rhythm.

2 Ask them to find English words with the same stress pattern as their name, or as their friends' names.

FOLLOW-UP 2

Encourage learners to indicate word stress in their notes, finding a way that suits *them*. Examples could be:

- underlining the syllable using a particular colour

  <u>con</u>sonant

- putting a (coloured) dot above or under the syllable

  c̣ȯnsonant

- writing the stressed syllable in a different script

  CON sonant

- representing the syllables by different shapes.

  consonant

You yourself should always clearly indicate the stressed syllable on the board. Personally, I like to draw a rectangle around the stressed syllable. If the syllable should also be slightly longer (because of the vowel, or because the consonant after the vowel is voiced), I draw an oval with a piece of coloured chalk.

Cuisinaire rods (rods used to teach how to count) are very useful to indicate stress, as they have different lengths and colours and can be manipulated. They are particularly helpful with very young learners who cannot write, as the 'shape' of the whole word can be represented and played with independently of the spelling.

FOLLOW-UP 3

1 Make word stress visible by using your students to make the 'shapes' of words. Weakly stressed (unstressed) syllables are represented by a student sitting down, stressed syllables by a student standing up.

2 Ask learners to stand up as they say the stressed syllable, and sit down for unstressed syllables. They can also walk word stress (see 2.1), putting their foot down strongly when they say the stressed syllable. Of course stress can always be clapped (see 2.7).

VARIATION

Select some short pieces of music with different rhythms for your students to choose from, or ask them to listen to their favourite music at home and find pieces where the rhythm fits the stress pattern you are working on. During the next lesson, your students discuss their findings in groups. Check that they have got the right stress pattern. They may bring in the music and practise saying words to the rhythm of the music.

COMMENTS

It is important to point out that pop music does not always follow the normal stress pattern of words. Bring in some examples and ask your learners to find more.

2.6 Feeling the rhythm

LEVEL

Elementary and above

TIME

5 minutes +

AIMS

Becoming aware of the rhythm of English

MATERIALS

A short poem or rhyme

PREPARATION

Find a short poem or rhyme which is easy to understand, preferably with repetitions.

PROCEDURE

Do this at the beginning of a lesson as a warmer.

1 The learners stand in circles of about 10 people. Ask them to take one step forward, swinging their arms from behind their backs to high in front of them and then step back, swinging their arms down. You can practise with one group first while the others watch.

2 Say the poem or rhyme, accompanying the rhythm with the movements.

3 The students imitate you. When they have got the rhythm (but before they get tired), proceed with the rest of your lesson.

FOLLOW-UP

Ask the learners to stand in a line behind each other and put one hand on the shoulder of the person in front. Ask them to close their eyes and sway forwards and backwards to the rhythm of a poem. Then they can take away their hand and go on moving to the rhythm of a text. It may help to tell them they are like rowers who have to row in unison. At a signal, they open their eyes to check they are still following the rhythm of the group, then close their eyes again and continue.

COMMENTS

This activity improves group dynamics, loosens up the students, and gets them to internalize the rhythm of the language.

Acknowledgements

I learnt the original idea during a seminar at the Kreisvolkshochschule in Gelnhausen (Germany) based on the work of Bernard Dufeu at Mainz University.

Suggestions for texts

The same texts as suggested in 'Speak rhythmically' (2.7) would do well here. I particularly like counting rhymes for this activity, such as:

> Icker backer, soldier cracker
> Icker backer boo
> Engine number nine
> Out go you!

Opie's *The Singing Game* (see Further Reading) has a whole chapter of songs usually sung with clapping, on a number of topics that lend themselves well to language learning (for example, 'I went to a Chinese restaurant', 'A sailor went to sea').

Lyrics from pop songs can also be used—ask your students to find some! Poems by contemporary poets in English can also provide interesting texts, for example, Lemn Sissay. Whenever possible, get your learners to compose the texts!

2.7 Speak rhythmically

LEVEL

All

TIME

5–10 minutes a lesson for several lessons

AIMS

Mastering rhythm progressively

Stage one: developing rhythm awareness

PREPARATION

Decide what two-syllable words or utterances you would like to practise, for example, 'Hello', 'Come on', 'Sit down', 'Who's there?', 'Goodbye', 'behind' (all with stress on the second syllable).

PROCEDURE

1 Ask your students if anything has struck them about the rhythm of English and other languages. You will hear comments like: 'The French, the Italians, and the Spaniards speak very quickly', 'Vietnamese has a very striking rhythm', etc.

2 Tell them that one of the basic rhythmic patterns of English is a two-syllable rhythm with a weak and a strong beat. Demonstrate by saying: 'Hello!' and clapping your hands.

3 Your students say 'Hello!' and beat the rhythm with their hands at the same time. For the weakly-stressed syllable they touch the ball of the thumb with the tip of their fingers, and for the strongly-stressed syllable they clap their hands.

4 They do this again, but without actually saying the word.

5 Make this a chain activity: you start clapping the rhythm and they follow, each in turn.

6 When your students can all do this with two-syllable words and phrases, move to stage two.

Stage two: mastering the rhythm of utterances through peer correction

PREPARATION

Think of some examples of simple conversational phrases for Step 2 below.

PROCEDURE

1 Tell the learners you are going to clap a simple phrase, such as 'Good morning!'. Ask one student to start from this and add a word or short phrase, but neither of you will speak.

2 Demonstrate:

Unspoken: (Good morning!)   ∪ — ∪

Unspoken: (Good morning, Mary.)   ∪ — ∪ — ∪

∪ indicates shorter syllables and — a longer syllable. The ' before a syllable indicates stress.

3 Get the others to clap the new phrase with the first student. When he or she is satisfied that everyone can do it, they all say the sentence aloud, and clap at the same time.

4 Ask the group whether the clapping fits the phrase. Point out any errors.

5 The class say the phrases and clap correctly, and then clap without speaking. Finally, get the first student to clap alone while the students in the group listen, thinking of the word.

VARIATION 1

1 To increase the sensation of rhythm, ask your students to clap their hands on their thighs.

2 The students face each other in pairs and clap their hands against their neighbours', only touching each other's hands when there is primary stress. (This is ideal for peer correction.)

VARIATION 2

To enable the students to feel the rhythm even more strongly, ask them to beat their hands flat on each other's backs.

FOLLOW-UP 1

Repeat this over a number of lessons, varying tne phrases, until all the learners can do it. Then they do it in groups of four, each person extending the clapped phrase or sentence in turn.

FOLLOW-UP 2

Encourage the students to recall the phrases, without moving, clapping, or speaking, just feeling the rhythm in themselves.

Stage three: reciting simple poems or rhymes expressively with the correct rhythm

PREPARATION

Choose a nursery rhyme or simple poem with a clear rhythm (see the suggestions in Further Reading). A couple of examples are given in Step 2 below.

PROCEDURE

1 Hand out the text of the rhyme you have chosen, or give it as a dictation. Imaginative ways of using dictations can be found in *Dictation: New Methods, New Possibilities* by Davis and Rinvolucri (1988).

2 Read out the rhyme or poem, and ask your students to clap the rhythm: first repeating the rhyme after you, then just clapping.

Examples

> Thirty days has September,
> April, June, and November,
> And all the rest have thirty-one,
> Except for February alone,
> Which has twenty-eight days clear,
> And twenty-nine in each leap year.
>
> traditional

> I never saw a purple cow,
> I never hope to see one;
> But I can tell you anyhow,
> I'd rather see than be one.
>
> Gelett Burgess

> I can't lose.
> Everything I do is right,
> I do it because it's right.
> It's right because I do it.
>
> I can't win.
> Everything I do is wrong,
> I do it because it's wrong.
> It's wrong because I do it.
>
> R. D. Laing

This last one is very stimulating—it introduces emphatic stress and is an excellent discussion starter in more advanced groups.

3 In pairs, the students stand face to face and clap each other's hands to the rhythm of the poem.

4 Now encourage your students to recite the rhymes or poems in pairs or groups and, finally, alone.

5 You can also ask your students to nod their heads, click their fingers, or tap to the rhythm, and even dance if you feel they are ready for this.

FOLLOW-UP 1   Encourage your students to compose their own poems and present them in class or to a partner as in the main procedure. This is an example written by a student:

> Good morning!
> How are you, darling?
> Fit as a starling!
> Better than the king!

FOLLOW-UP 2   Once you are satisfied your students can clap the rhythms of simple poems, get them to 'clap' or 'beat' the rhythm of a simple dialogue *mentally*. In other words, they practise the rhythm in their heads and start talking while the rhythm is fresh in their minds. This is the last stage before spontaneous practice. It is also an excellent silent preparation before reading a text or reciting a poem. Also encourage your students to do this when learning short texts by heart.

FOLLOW-UP 3   After this, add pauses, pitch differences, and tone of voice.

2.8 Rhythm round

LEVEL   **All**

TIME   **15–20 minutes**

AIMS   **Raising awareness of rhythm patterns in English and internalizing them progressively**

PROCEDURE

1 Explain the general idea of how rounds work. There are four lines. The singers start at intervals of one line, repeat the words and music a specified number of times, and finish in the order they started in.

2 Teach your students a simple round, for example, 'London's burning'. Rehearse the words and tune. When they can sing it straight through, divide the class into four groups. Tell the groups you want them to sing it through twice in succession but starting one after the other: group two starts when group one reaches the second line, group three when group one is at the third line and group two at the second, and so on.

3 Now, get your students to repeat the round, but with just the words—no music. This is now a *rhythm round*. You can ask them to do it in different voices—for example, one normal, one nearly whispering.

Here is 'London's burning' written as a rhythm round. Each of these ♩ is twice as long as one of these ♪ , which is twice as long as one of these ♪ . I have also indicated where the main stressed syllables fall like this: '.

London's burning

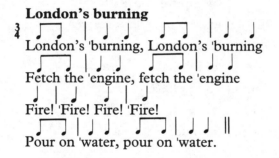

London's 'burning, London's 'burning

Fetch the 'engine, fetch the 'engine

Fire! 'Fire! Fire! 'Fire!

Pour on 'water, pour on 'water.

FOLLOW-UP 1

1 Present this new rhythm round.

Fish 'n' chips

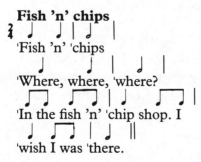

'Fish 'n' 'chips

'Where, where, 'where?

'In the fish 'n' 'chip shop. I

'wish I was 'there.

Read it right through, then get the class to repeat it after you a line at a time. Ask them to repeat it several times after you. You can change your voice: for example, normal speaking voice, shouting, whispering, very high pitch, very low pitch, normal voice again. If necessary, do further repetition work on pairs of lines until the class have memorized the whole round.

2 Put them back into their four groups and do the round twice,

each group starting and finishing a line apart. Repeat. If you have difficulty keeping your students to the rhythm, clap on the accented beats and get them to clap with you. This makes it almost impossible to go against the rhythm.

Make rhythm rounds a regular element of rhythm training in your class.

FOLLOW-UP 2

1 Ask students to change the words of some rounds (see 2.11, 'Write your own song'), invent your own, or encourage your students to write rhythm rounds. They must have four (or eight) lines, each with two main stressed syllables. The end of lines two and four should rhyme. Don't worry if the words are slightly nonsensical—it adds to the fun.

2 You can include a structure/function you are working on. Follow Step 3 above (in an eight-line round, have the groups start at two-line intervals). Here is an eight-line round to practise past simple questions and negative forms. The stressed syllables are marked thus: '

For your 'breakfast this 'morning
        'What did you 'eat?
Did you 'have any   'porridge?
Did you 'have any   'meat?
      I 'didn't have   'porridge
    And I 'didn't have   'meat
    I had 'tea with   'sugar
    But 'nothing to   'eat.

COMMENTS

Singing or saying rounds raises the energy level in the class, an important benefit on cold, wet, hot, sleepy, boring days, and helps internalize rhythm.

Acknowledgements

1 I owe this activity to David Cranmer.

2 The round 'Fish 'n' chips' is based on the anonymous round 'Banbury Ale' in the Ravenscroft collection *Pammelia*, London, 1609.

2.9 Talking hands

LEVEL

All

TIME

10–15 minutes the first time, 5 minutes in further lessons

| AIMS | **Learning to recognize rhythm, internalizing the rhythm of simple utterances, associating rhythm with meaning** |

MATERIALS   **Desks (optional)**

PROCEDURE

1 Tell your students that in many countries of Africa and Polynesia, people communicate with drums or gongs, simply by beating the rhythm. (For our purpose, we disregard the fact that there is often a difference of pitch as well.) By this means they transmit a limited number of messages over long distances. Tell your class that in English too, rhythm is important, and that they are going to communicate like talking drums or gongs, but using their hands instead.

2 Make a list on the board of simple utterances that they know and number them, for example, (1) *Hello* (2) *Good morning* (3) *Goodbye* (4) *How are you?*, including some expressions of praise such as (5) *Wonderful!*, and (6) *Oh dear!* Demonstrate how to clap the rhythms (see 2.7, stage one, page 50).

3 Clap the rhythm of one of the words or phrases and ask the class to recognize which one you are clapping. Check by asking your students to write down the corresponding number. Do this with all the utterances you have chosen, until they can do it easily.

4 Ask your students to do the same in pairs.

5 Divide the class into two groups (villages) and appoint a chief and a number of 'drummers' for each village. The rest of the class are villagers who will overhear the message. The chiefs position themselves with one of their drummers at each end of the classroom. One chief orders his 'drummer' to transmit a message to a relay drummer who then transmits it to another until the message reaches the chief at the other end of the classroom. The second chief says, 'The chief from the other village is saying "Good morning"', for example. If this is right, the drummers and villages clap 'Wonderful!' or another expression of praise. If the interpretation is wrong, they clap 'Oh dear!' and make a surprised or sceptical face.

6 The second chief answers the message in the same way.

7 Go on doing this with basic utterances over a number of weeks or months.

VARIATION 1

Use this technique to teach new words and phrases. Before asking learners to pronounce them, get them to clap the stress pattern to each other, then to clap and speak. Or ask half of the class to clap, and the other half to speak.

VARIATION 2

Beat the rhythm on desks, using the tips of the fingers for minor stress and the palms of the hands for major stress, or if you can, use tambourines, drums, xylophones, or glockenspiels (see 2.17, 'Speak musically').

VARIATION 3   Teach your students to clap their names to each other. Group them according to the stress patterns of their names. Organize a competition to see if they can recognize the names.

VARIATION 4   Ask your students to write down where they come from: 'Peter's from London', etc. In small groups (4–6) they clap the messages, saying them as well. Then they clap but say nothing, and the other learners try to recognize the message.

VARIATION 5   Many of the messages transmitted in Africa are praise poems. Ask your students to compose short, amusing praise utterances about each other, for example, 'William the conqueror', 'Edward the bold', 'Maria the smiler', 'Peter the magnificent'. These praise sentences can be clapped, beaten, or played now and then to encourage a student who has done something particularly well, or simply as a warmer.

VARIATION 6   Go on asking your students to make sentences to clap and transmit as described above, within the context of your lessons. For example, if the topic is food, ask them to make sentences such as 'Oliver likes bananas', 'Frédéric prefers peaches', etc., and proceed as above.

FOLLOW-UP   When your class can do this easily, do 2.21, 'Whistle/hum the message', where the same principle is extended to intonation.

2.10 Sentence stress

LEVEL   **Elementary and above (except very young learners)**

TIME   **Three stages of 15–20 minutes (can be in separate lessons)**

AIMS   **Raising awareness of how stress affects the meaning of a sentence**

MATERIALS   **Rhymes and statements (see Preparation)**

PREPARATION   1 Your students need to know what word stress is before you do this.

2 Prepare a class set of two suitable rhymes at your students' level such as 'This is the house that Jack built' (Opie 1951: 229) or 'Girls and boys come out to play' (Opie 1951: 99). Rhymes which contain several one-syllable words are the most suitable.

3 Prepare statements as shown in stage three of Procedure.

Note

The traditional term 'sentence stress' is used here to refer to what is really prominence within tone units, of which there may be several in a sentence.

Stage one: noticing stress

PROCEDURE

1 Teach your class the first rhyme. First say it a couple of times, then sing it if you know the tune. Check that your students understand it.

2 Ask them to clap the rhythm, or move any part of their body they like (head, a leg, a hand, a finger) when they feel a strong stress as you say the rhyme.

3 Encourage the students to say it aloud if they want, or else to say it to themselves as you are saying it, still clapping the rhythm or moving some part of their body.

4 Ask your learners how many syllables the words have. Remind them (or elicit) that two-syllable words have one syllable stressed more strongly than the other, and ask them to observe what happens in words which have one syllable only. Are any words stressed more strongly than the others? Ask them to read the text again, and underline the syllables which have stronger stress, if any.

5 Go through the text, asking your students to say where they feel there is strong stress. Settle any disagreements and ask if they can find a rule to determine which words need stronger stress. (They will probably find that verbs, nouns, adjectives, and adverbs have stronger stress.) One way to help them to discover this is by asking if they can see what all the words that are lightly stressed (unstressed) have in common. (These are often known as 'function', 'grammatical', or 'tool' words, and are pronounced using weak forms—see 3.13.)

6 Say or sing the rhyme together, then ask the students to say it to each other in pairs, preferably standing, remaining aware of the stress and rhythm. Encourage them to nod, tap, etc. as they say it to each other. The partners give feedback while you monitor. Gently provide the right stress if needed. They change partners a couple of times.

7 Ask your class to say the rhyme inwardly, still being very aware of the rhythm inside themselves.

VARIATION

In Step 2, make sentence stress visible by asking your students to stand in for words. Write a sentence on the board. Put as many chairs in front of the board as there are words. Students sit on the chairs when the word is weakly stressed (unstressed), and stand when it is strongly stressed. Each student says the word he or she represents with the right stress, for example, 'There are no BIRDS [standing] in the classroom'.

Stage two: contrastive/emphatic stress

1 Teach your class the second rhyme. Say the first stanza and ask them to repeat it. Check that they understand it. Then write it on the board.

2 Ask them to say it while clapping the stressed syllables. For example:

THIS is the HOUSE that JACK BUILT.

3 Ask a student to indicate the main stress on the board (see 2.5, page 47).

4 If you can, also ask your learners to walk to the rhythm of the sentence, putting their foot down strongly when there is primary stress. Students who have a problem should do this with a student who finds it easy. It is best if they walk to the rhythm and say the sentence at the same time.

5 Draw your students' attention to the fact that one word is stressed more strongly than the others. Ask them why they think this is.

6 Ask some students to repeat the rhyme, clap it, walk it, putting the main stress on a different word, for example:

This IS the HOUSE that JACK BUILT.

Ask them what difference they feel there is. They should normally find there is a difference in stress and meaning. Ask them to build a context around this new way of saying the line (for example, 'This is definitely the house that Jack built, there is no doubt about it.').

7 Proceed like this with at least three or four stanzas of the rhyme.

8 In pairs, the students say the two versions of each line alternately to practise the difference, for example:

THIS is the HOUSE that JACK BUILT.
This IS the HOUSE that JACK BUILT.

For learners who cannot yet write English, proceed as in the Variation in stage one, but the learners sit on the floor next to their chairs so that there are three 'levels': floor, chair, standing. They start sitting on the floor and change if necessary according to the degree of stress.

Do this regularly in other lessons, asking your students to change words to fit the sentence stress, add further verses, or adapt or update rhymes, for example:

This is the car that Jack bought.

This is the purse
That lay in the car
That Jack bought.

This is the thief
That stole the purse
That lay in the car
That Jack bought.

See also 2.11, 'Write your own song'.

Stage three: practising in conversations

At this stage class practice is beginning to be more communicative. You can concentrate on sentence stress only, or you may want to combine it with intonation practice as well.

PREPARATION

Prepare a series of statements about your students, the school, their workplace, current affairs, etc., at a level and on topics appropriate for your group. Some should be true and some should be false.

Examples

I suppose Joe watched a football match yesterday.
The weather is very hot today.
Spiders have twelve legs.
Spaghetti comes from Iceland.
Inflation is what happens when prices go up.
Horses don't fly in winter.

PROCEDURE

1 Ask the learners to show whether these statements are true or false by repeating them, replacing some words and making careful use of stress. For example:

Joe watched a VOLLEYBALL game yesterday.
Horses don't fly at ALL.
Yes, the weather IS very hot today.

2 Ask your students to prepare their own list of true or false statements. In pairs, one student reads out one of their statements, and the other student responds as in Step 1. They can change partners a couple of times. Monitor, but ask students to give feedback on their partner's performance.

VARIATION

For intermediate and advanced learners

1 Tell your class anecdotes with surprising facts and ask them to write down what they think is true/false.

2 They discuss in pairs, using stress to explain their views.

3 The students ask you precise questions about elements of the story, for example:

Did the man actually fall from the FOURTEENTH floor?
Yes, he fell from the FOURTEENTH floor.

4 Encourage the students to prepare a similar story that they can practise in pairs during another lesson.

FOLLOW-UP 1

Word order can also be used to show emphasis, for example:

It is pears I like, not plums.
Pears I like, but plums I don't.
What I like is pears, not plums.

This provides a context for practice in pairs. One student uses just stress to highlight a point and the other responds by using word order. For example:

A: I usually drink TEA for breakfast.
B: So it is tea you drink, not coffee.
A: That's right.

A: I usually drink tea for BREAKFAST.
B: What you drink for breakfast is tea, but what about supper?

You can also include nonsensical situations, for example:

C: I like drinking coffee in a HAT.
D: Really? I prefer drinking MILK in a hat.

FOLLOW-UP 2

In twos or threes, the students pretend that they are in a noisy place, for example a railway station or busy street, or trying to talk on a bad phone line. One starts a conversation, another 'misunderstands' and puts the stress on the wrong word/syllable. The other students correct them by stressing the right word even more strongly.

2.11 Write your own song

LEVEL

Elementary and above

TIME

20 minutes + in the first lesson (depending on length and difficulty of song), another 20 minutes + at home, 10–15 minutes in the second lesson

AIMS

Raising awareness of stress and rhythm, noticing unstressed syllables, pronouncing weak forms

MATERIALS

A class set of the words of a song chosen according to your learners' age and background; recording of the song (optional)

PREPARATION

Prepare a song. Many traditional songs are appropriate, and nursery rhymes are also a good source. Limericks are also very appropriate for this kind of activity, but they are not sung. See Further Reading for suggestions of sources.

Lesson one

PROCEDURE

1 Hand out the words of the song. Teach your students to sing it.

2 Ask them to indicate word stress, for example, by underlining or highlighting the stressed syllables:

> WHAT shall we DO with the DRUNKen SAIlor?

3 Ask the learners to change the words of one line, but keeping the same rhythmic pattern: they must be able to sing it easily. They may ask you or each other for vocabulary, or use a dictionary if needed.

> WHAT shall we DO with the LAzy STUdent?

4 Get them to try out the new version with a partner. Help them to sort out any difficulties, which are usually due to wrong stressing.

5 Ask your students to rewrite a stanza or the whole song for the next lesson.

Lesson two

6 Ask your students to try out their new versions in pairs. If any students have a rhythmically acceptable version, encourage them to sing it to the whole class, or to a small group. Help out students who have problems, and encourage them to re-work their texts for the next lesson.

FOLLOW-UP 1

1 Choose a slightly more difficult song for the same activity. Further verses from 'What shall we do with the drunken sailor?', for example, have difficult vocabulary and some lines with more syllables than others, which still have to be sung to the same rhythm:

> TAKE him and SHAKE him and TRY to aWAKE him ...
> PULL out the LONG boat and WET him all OVer ...
> PUT him in the SCUPPers with a HOSE-pipe ON him ...
> TIE him to the TAFFrail when she's YARD arm UNder ...

After singing the song, ask the students to practise saying the words without singing, but keeping the same rhythm.

2 Ask your students to produce alternative words for the difficult lines too, with the same number of syllables and stressed and unstressed syllables in exactly the same places.

FOLLOW-UP 2

1 Ask your students to make up a text they can sing, with the same number of stressed syllables, but with more unstressed syllables. They should still be able to sing it to the same rhythm and within the same time span as the original version:

> PUT him in the SCULLery with the DIRty DISHes ...

2 They check by singing together in pairs: one of the two sings the original, the other the new version, but they must finish together. You can also ask them to provide variations using vocabulary linked with a particular topic you have been studying.

Do the same with simple utterances from the learners' textbooks. Ask them to keep the same overall rhythmic pattern but to add unstressed syllables. They then practise in pairs, trying to say the two versions within the same time span. Always do this in a playful atmosphere and do not place too much importance on complete success—the objective is to pronounce weakly stressed words and weak forms more quickly.

Some appropriate traditional songs

What shall we do with the drunken sailor?
Happy birthday to you
The little drummer boy
The twelve days of Christmas.

'Folk' songs and country music songs are often suitable, for example by Woody Guthrie, Bob Dylan, Joan Baez, Pete Seeger, Johnny Cash.

Examples of student variations

Original nursery rhyme:

Baa, baa, black sheep,
Have you any wool?
Yes, sir, yes, sir,
Three bags full.
One for my master,
And one for my dame,
And one for the little boy
Who lives down the lane.

New version:

Helen, my friend	Jane, Jane, my friend,
Could you find the way?	Can we find our way?
Yes Jo, that's sure	Yes, John, that's sure,
I'll find the way.	We have maps.
I'll take my rucksack	One for your children
And I'll take the map,	And one for your wife
But it quickly blows away	And one for the nicest guide
And I can't find the way.	Who likes to do his best.

(Claude, 18)

Original nursery rhyme:

Oh where, oh where has my little dog gone?
Oh where, oh where can he be?
With his ears cut short, and his tail cut long
Oh where, oh where can he be?

New versions:

Oh why, oh why are there so many wars?
Oh why, oh why do they fight?

Why do they not see there is too much blood?
Oh why, oh why do they fight?

(Laurence, 18)

Oh where, oh where has my own head gone?
Oh where, oh where can it be?
With my little pink cheeks, my blue and green wig
Oh where, oh where can it be?

(Françoise, 19)

COMMENTS

This activity helps learners to obtain insight into how word stress contributes to rhythm or 'beat', in songs as well as in speech.

2.12 Eat your words!

LEVEL

All

TIME

5–10 minutes

AIMS

Helping students to pronounce weak forms

MATERIALS

Recordings of authentic spoken texts, a class set of transcripts

PREPARATION

Select a few 30-second recordings of authentic spoken texts with plenty of weak forms, that your students can understand easily.

PROCEDURE

1 Hand out the transcripts and play the recording. Ask your students to listen and underline the words that they hear are 'eaten' by the speakers. Show how words can be 'eaten': /sm/ for 'some', /bt/ for 'but', and /n/ for 'and', for example.

2 Pair off the students. If possible, put students who have difficulty with this aspect of pronunciation with those who do not. Ask them to check if they have heard the same words being 'eaten'. Monitor, and settle any disagreements.

3 Play the recording again and ask the class to focus on some or all of the 'eaten' words.

4 The students practise using either the transcript or a simple rhyme or limerick. They cross out the words they are going to 'eat'. Then they say the text, 'eating' the words they have crossed out.

The following example illustrates how to 'eat' *to* and *but*:

Nothing to do but work,
        Nothing to eat but food,
Nothing to wear but clothes,
        To keep one from going nude.

Nothing to comb but hair,
  Nowhere to sleep but in bed,
Nothing to weep but tears,
  Nothing to bury but dead.

from 'The Pessimist' (Benjamin Franklin King)

FOLLOW-UP 1

Your students may enjoy writing their own amusing texts with words to 'eat'.

FOLLOW-UP 2

Have a contest to find the best 'word eater'. Students come and read or recite a text with lots of words to 'eat'. The class gives a prize to the best 'word eater'.

FOLLOW-UP 3

Go on teaching your students to 'eat' more words, until all the weak forms have been dealt with.

COMMENTS

This activity helps beginners to learn to pronounce weak forms. You can also use it with more advanced learners who have a tendency to pronounce all words with the same emphasis, as it will help them put less emphasis on weakly stressed words or syllables.

2.13 With the speed of summer lightning

LEVEL

Elementary and above

TIME

10–15 minutes

AIMS

Learning to make liaisons, helping students to pronounce weak forms

MATERIALS

A recording of a short text your students need not really understand

PREPARATION

This activity is best done when your learners have gained confidence and when they have a reasonable mastery of the stress, rhythm, and intonation of English.

PROCEDURE

1 Play the tape, and ask the class how many breaks they can hear between words.

2 Discuss, and point out that there are very few breaks between words in English because all the words are normally linked when speaking. This means it helps to take large breaths.

3 Ask the students to sit comfortably and do a breathing exercise as described in 1.1C.

4 Working in pairs, the students speak without stopping for 15 seconds, saying as many words as possible. If they link words together and use weak forms they will be able to say more. They can *read* a text the first time they do this. Their partner provides feedback on how well they linked and used weak forms.

5 Gradually lengthen the time they speak without stopping. Remind them of the best places to pause if they need to (between 'tone units' or thought groups).

6 Organize a contest. In small groups one student tries to speak for as long as possible without stopping. The others try to do better.

FOLLOW-UP 1

To avoid giving the impression that speaking quickly is essential, combine this activity with 2.2, 'Slow down'. Ask them to speak slowly for 30 seconds, 'fast' for another 30 seconds, and 'normally' for 30 seconds again.

FOLLOW-UP 2

In pairs or groups, students take it in turns to speak at different speeds. The listeners note down what happens to intelligibility and accuracy of pronunciation and discuss their impressions. In this way the speakers get the feel of the speed that suits them *and* English. Then discuss with your students which types of activities could be done speaking quickly or more slowly.

COMMENTS

This complements 'Slow down!' (2.2) and 'Pause!' (2.4). See also 'Write your own song' (2.11) and 'Eat your words!' (2.12), which deal with weak forms.

2.14 Move to the tune of English

LEVEL

All

TIME

10–15 minutes

AIMS

Making students aware of the intonation of English and internalizing pitch movements

MATERIALS

Recordings of music and texts

PREPARATION

Select musical excerpts (see the suggestions below) and recordings of poetry and prose.

Use this activity when the students have an awareness of the rhythm of English (see 2.1, for example).

PROCEDURE

1 Ask your learners to sit comfortably, or if possible to stand anywhere they like in the classroom.

2 Tell them that you are going to play some music and that you want them to concentrate on the melody, moving their heads following the ups and downs of the music. Play one to two minutes of the music.

3 Play it again. The students 'conduct', moving their arms and hands to the music.

4 Now read or play the class a poem. They move their arms and hands, following the melody of the language. They need not understand the text. In monolingual classes do the same with a poem in their mother tongue for comparison.

5 Invite the class to comment on their sensations of these intonation movements.

6 Ask them to try and recreate these sensations during conversation classes.

VARIATION

With short spoken texts, ask your students to breathe in when the intonation rises, and out when it falls.

FOLLOW-UP 1

1 To get students to overcome their negative feelings about English intonation, ask them to relax and breathe calmly (see 1.1B, C, and Variation) and listen to the tune of the language. Closing their eyes will improve their concentration.

2 Put the learners into pairs and read or play a text.

3 Ask the learners to slowly open their eyes and in pairs to discuss their impressions of how English intonation sounds to them. Listen unobtrusively. Change the partners and get those who have a very negative impression to exchange their views with someone who has a more positive view.

4 Try to do this again in later lessons with recordings of different voices and people in a variety of situations. Monitor carefully so that you can decide on what action to take in future lessons.

COMMENTS

1 2.15, 'English babbling', is a good follow-up to this.

2 This gets your learners to internalize the specific pitch movements of utterances they are learning, to associate them with context, meaning, attitudes, etc. Brazil 1985, Cruttenden 1986, and Roach 1983 in Further Reading contain further guidance on this. It is important to organize activities in which the learners will be able to practise the pitch movements in a fairly natural way. Drama activities and role plays lend themselves well to practising intonation for introducing or ending a topic, indicating your partner is expected to take his or her turn in a conversation, and to denoting social roles. See 2.25, 'Tales', and *Role Play* (Porter-Ladousse 1987) and *Drama* (Wessels 1987) in this series for ideas.

Suggestions for music

Choose music which has a striking melody. Slow music is best. Excerpts of one to two minutes will do, for example:

- J. S. Bach: Sonata in C minor for flute and violin, basso continuo BWV 1079, no. 8 (the first and third movements)
- Handel: *Music for the Royal Fireworks*, the largo ('La Paix') or one of the minuets
- Vaughan Williams: 'Fantasia on Greensleeves'
- New Age music: there is plenty to choose from. It is best not to use synthesizer music all the time
- Any instrumental version of a traditional English-language song or pop song that is striking because of its melody, not because of its beat! For example, 'Early one morning' or 'Skye Boat Song'.

2.15 English babbling

LEVEL	**All**
TIME	**5–10 minutes**
AIMS	**Approaching English intonation in a non-threatening way**
MATERIALS	**Any two-minute recording in English**

PREPARATION
It is essential to do 2.14 first because students need to have become aware of the intonation of English and to have internalized pitch movements.

PROCEDURE
1 Get your students to relax and do the Variation of 1.1. They should listen to the intonation only.

2 In pairs, the learners say anything they like in their mother tongue, but imitating what they consider to be English intonation (and gestures, etc.). They discuss how it feels to speak their mother tongue with this alien intonation. Try to get them to be as specific as possible.

3 The partners tell each other how convincing they thought their rendering of English intonation was.

4 Later ask them to do the same when speaking English.

COMMENTS
Do this as a 'warmer' before pronunciation or conversation activities. See also 3.1 and 1.12.

2.16 Fireworks

LEVEL	**All**
TIME	**5–10 minutes**
AIMS	**Developing awareness of intonation**
PROCEDURE	**1** Ask the students to play with intonation in pairs or groups. Ask them to choose a vowel and move up and down with their voices while saying it. They should start from as low as possible and move to as high as possible, then start as high as possible and move down in a variety of ways. Draw some possibilities on the board:

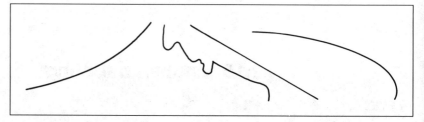

2 Associate pitch movements with other impressions, such as a firework rising and falling in the sky, a plane taking off and landing, or a bird soaring.

3 The students think of more pitch movements they can make with their voices. In pairs, they ask each other to make them. For example: 'Say /e/ as if it was a leaf moving in the wind.'

4 Ask the learners to say some sentences in their mother tongue or English with some of these pitch movements and to express how it feels. Learners have said things like: 'It gives me a feeling of pleasure.' 'It is ironical.' 'It sounds angry.'

5 The students think of music or other sounds (mechanical or natural) with pitch changes that they think English intonation sounds like. This can be done as homework. They talk about their ideas in groups in the next lesson.

COMMENTS	This is a good 'warmer' at the beginning of lessons.

2.17 Speak musically

LEVEL	**All**
TIME	**10–20 minutes**
AIMS	**From rhythm to pitch and intonation**

MATERIALS

A xylophone or glockenspiel (two for a larger group). Simple alternatives to these instruments are described below. Recordings of simple utterances (optional)

COMMENTS

This activity is particularly useful in helping learners to pronounce weak forms properly and to contract in the right places. Learners of all ages like it for the insight they gain into the way the English language works.

Select the stages you consider appropriate for the needs of your students. This activity is particularly useful for speakers of Asian languages such as Thai, Khmer, and Vietnamese.

PREPARATION

If you do not have a xylophone or glockenspiel, you can simply use three or four pieces of wood or metal tubes of different lengths, thicknesses, or diameter, hung from strings or placed on the floor or on a simple stand (two bars of wood), and two sticks to play them with.

Glass bottles containing different quantities of water can also be used. The students can help make the instruments.

Stage one

PROCEDURE

1 Place the instrument in the middle of the classroom. To warm up your students hit notes, and encourage them to respond by tapping their desks in reply. This will give them the feel of the instrument, and get them ready for the activities below.

2 To develop awareness of rhythm, play the rhythm of a simple two-syllable word with stress on the first syllable, such as 'orange', 'coffee', or 'bigger'. Using one note, beat more strongly for the first than for the second, which should be shorter and softer. Repeat this several times, using a different note and emphasizing the rhythm with arm movements. To make sure you are following the correct rhythm, say it in your head at the same time. Encourage your students to do the same.

3 Play the rhythm again and say the word aloud, for example, 'orange'. Silently gesture that anyone in the group can have a go.

4 Play the rhythm again and ask the learners to say 'orange' together. You yourself are now silent.

5 Repeat Steps 1–3, using a word with stress on the final syllable.

6 Play a game in which you or a student plays a rhythm and the class suggest a word which fits. Then progress to short phrases.

Stage two: higher and lower pitch, jumps up and down

PROCEDURE

1 Make sure the class cannot see what notes you are playing this time. Play jumps of two notes on your instrument: C–F, F–C, both fast and slow. Play both falling and rising sequences, and ask the class if they can hear the difference. Allow students

who cannot distinguish a rising sequence from a falling one to actually see the instrument and encourage them to play it themselves.

2 Once they know how to distinguish them, ask students to play either rising or falling sequences. The other students demonstrate how they perceive it: for example, when the tune is falling they sit down, and when it is rising they raise an arm. Now and then one should play the same sequence twice, but once loudly and once softly to help them understand the difference between loudness and pitch.

3 Play words or phrases you have recorded, or say them yourself. Ask your students to recognize which ones have falling intonation and which ones rising. Some of them should be said at the same pitch, but with one syllable louder.

FOLLOW-UP

In the coming weeks your students try to notice different kinds of rising and falling intonation. Get them to use different pitch in appropriate contexts and to learn to associate it with meaning, speed, pause, tone of voice, etc.

COMMENTS

This is one simple example of how to approach pitch with the help of musical instruments. Recorders, penny whistles, and keyboards can also be used.

2.18 The robot

LEVEL   All

TIME   5–10 minutes

AIMS   Learning not to go up and down with one's voice too much

PREPARATION Prepare a list of fairly short phrases such as instructions or reports of the kind that robots might say. For younger learners think of the voices in computer games.

PROCEDURE   1 If you have a recording of a simple computer voice or of a robot or an electronic toy, allow your learners to listen to it and give them an opportunity to describe what they hear. If you have nothing suitable, imitate it yourself.

2 Tell the class that this is the best such machines can do, but that they are intelligible, even if such flat, monotonous voices are not very pleasant to listen to.

3 Each student picks out one of the short texts you have prepared, then moves about the room, meeting other robots and delivering their message. Listen and encourage the 'best'

robots—those whose voices do not move up and down at all. Allow the best ones to perform in front of the whole class.

FOLLOW-UP 1	Go on devoting a couple of minutes to this at the beginning of lessons for some time.
FOLLOW-UP 2	When the students can pronounce such utterances without too many undesirable pitch movements, ask them to improvise their own additions to the messages. Eventually do not give them any texts; ask them to improvise entirely.
FOLLOW-UP 3	When you feel they are ready, introduce nuclear tones (places where the voice moves up and down) into the messages. Then proceed to work on normal pitch and intonation.
VARIATION	1 With learners who cannot yet write, prepare four simple utterances that are easy to remember. 2 Teach them orally. 3 Divide the class into four groups and give each group one of the utterances. The learners move about and say their utterances when they meet someone. 4 Repeat with four other utterances.
COMMENTS	This activity is extremely helpful for people who have a tendency to use an intonation that goes up and down in an un-English fashion. It is particularly useful for speakers of tone languages or languages where the move up and down is not as tied to meaning and the attitude of the speaker as in English.

2.19 Musical words

LEVEL	All
TIME	5–10 minutes + some work at home
AIMS	**Practising different pitches as preparation for intonation work**
PREPARATION	For homework, ask your students to prepare a list of words containing a vowel or diphthong you want them to practise. As an extra challenge, request a variety of spellings of the target sound. Example: *first, search, word, burn, deter, pearl.* With very young learners, ask them to say four words with the sound in: 'Give me a word with /uː/ like in "shoe".'
PROCEDURE	1 Ask your students for some of the words they have found at

home. From these words, write the ones that they find difficult to pronounce on the board. Practise them, paying particular attention to the rhythm.

2 Divide your class into groups (four at most). Choose a leader for each. Explain they are going to sing the words like a round (see 2.8), but each group sings on a pitch chosen by the leader.

3 Get each group to start five seconds after the previous one.

4 Repeat, using different pitches.

FOLLOW-UP

In subsequent lessons they can make up short exchanges to sing in pairs, or in two groups, for example:

> A: Bye bye!
> B: Oh why!

2.20 Speak Fallese

LEVEL

All

TIME

15 minutes in one lesson, + 5 minutes each in several more lessons

AIMS

Learning different pitch movements and associating them with meaning

PREPARATION

Prepare nonsense utterances with English syllables and some short sentences. Choose syllables and words with open vowels such as /æ/ as in 'mash', /ʌ/ as in 'cut', /ɑː/ as in 'bar', and /ɒ/ as in 'dog'. See the examples in the Procedure.

PROCEDURE

1 Tell your class (or elicit from them) that in many languages the voice can move up and down on each syllable. This pitch movement changes the meaning of the syllable/word.

2 Tell them that they are going to speak a language where there is always a falling pitch. Show them how to distinguish low falls from low rises by whistling or using a swanee whistle (slide flute). With a swanee whistle they can actually see your hand moving up and down—if you do not have one, you can move your hand. Then ask them to distinguish between the pitch movements without seeing your hand move.

3 Write a nonsense utterance on the board in a way that illustrates the low fall, for example:

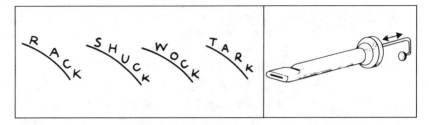

Say it rhythmically with a low falling intonation on each syllable. With young learners, make sure they can say it by heart before you move to step 4.

4 The learners practise in pairs, making falling movements with their hands at first. Listen in to see how well they do. They change partners.

5 Ask the learners to invent other nonsense utterances and 'talk' to each other in 'Fallese'.

6 At the beginning of the next lesson, give the learners five minutes to speak 'Fallese' Use simple utterances with actual English words, with the same kinds of vowels at first. Next include other vowels as well. Do this as a warmer for a few days.

7 Practise short nonsense utterances without breaks between the 'words' (syllables), and with a fall on the last syllable only. Make sure the last syllable contains an open vowel. For example:

Sopwagshuckwarf   Dishouldnotarg

8 Use real English phrases or sentences, and elicit from the learners in what situations they would use a low falling pitch contour. Practise doing the activity with these.

FOLLOW-UP

Do the same with 'Risese', using low rising intonation. At first make up nonsense words and use words with half-open and half-close vowels: /e/, /ɪ/, /ɔ:/, and /u:/. Then move to 'High Risese', first using vowels such as /i:/, /ɪ/, and /u:/. Other intonation contours can be introduced using the same approach.

2.21 Whistle/hum the message

LEVEL

All

TIME

5–10 minutes

AIMS

Recognizing the tunes of simple utterances; communicating by whistling or humming

PREPARATION

Do this when your students can do 2.9, 'Talking hands'.

PROCEDURE

1 Tell your class that it is possible to communicate just by whistling or humming an utterance. Tell them they are going to do this with simple utterances in class. If they cannot whistle they can hum instead.

2 Write a numbered list of simple utterances on the board. These can be simple formulae for greeting or leave taking to begin with. Choose utterances that are quite different from each other, and make sure they have different lengths as well as different intonation contours. Use a natural, friendly intonation.

3 Read them, hum them, and whistle them, making sure you keep the intonation and rhythm consistent. (You could also use a swanee whistle as in 2.20.)

4 Ask the class to imitate you. Next hum/whistle one of the utterances and ask the class to write down the number. Then tell them which one you were actually humming/whistling. Do this a couple of times if necessary.

5 Now ask your students to do this in pairs.

6 Practise this by dividing your class into two groups with messengers who transmit a message from one end of the class to the other.

FOLLOW-UP

Once your students have got the idea of this, it will only take one or two minutes. In future lessons, gradually lengthen the utterances and reduce the differences between them. Eventually the only difference will be the intonation and the attitude, for example, 'Good morning!' said in a friendly or an ironic manner. Dialogues from textbooks could be used.

2.22 The moods of English

LEVEL

All

TIME

20 minutes +

AIMS

Recognizing moods; associating moods with body language, voice quality, and intonation; acquiring the intonation of English within the general context of communication

MATERIALS

Video recordings of different native speakers expressing different moods; a class set of transcripts

PREPARATION

1 Prepare a short video recording of passages spoken by native speakers in up to three different moods: for example, happy,

enthusiastic, melancholy, angry, sad. If you cannot use a video, you yourself should act so that your students can associate the body language with the mood, voice quality, and intonation.

2 Prepare a set of transcripts of the video, or if this is linguistically too complex for your students, prepare some simpler short exchanges reflecting the same moods.

PROCEDURE

This activity helps learners recognize the moods of the people speaking to them, even if they do not understand the actual words. It is best done after 2.21, 'Whistle/hum the message'.

1 Prepare your students to listen attentively. You can do this by getting them to do a simple relaxation activity as suggested in 1.1B.

2 Tell your class they are going to watch a video of native speakers. The important point is to perceive the mood of the speakers. Give them a list of moods, including those you want them to recognize.

3 Play the recordings. If they have problems recognizing the moods at first, say some of the utterances yourself, exaggerating the moods with your face and body.

4 Give out the scripts. Choose one of the moods and ask your students to act the dialogue but with straight, expressionless faces and without moving their body at all.

5 Show the video of the chosen mood again. Discuss how the mood can be recognized.

6 Then ask your students in pairs to imitate the gestures, the body language, the tone of voice, and the intonation used in the video, feeling the mood expressed.

VARIATION

1 Select a video with, for example, four characters, and make copies of the script.

2 Divide your class into groups of four. Hand out the script. One learner in each group concentrates on the attitude and intonation of one character, who they will have to imitate afterwards.

3 The students who observed the same character join in groups to discuss what intonation is typical of that character. They practise parts of the dialogue, imitating the character they have focused on.

4 Pairs of students prepare new dialogues to act out afterwards, imitating the characteristic intonation of the character they observed originally. They play their dialogue to another pair, who try to guess who they are imitating. Then they discuss the effect of each character's intonation and what they need to do to imitate him or her.

COMMENTS	By doing this every now and again, changing models all the time, the students internalize intonation in all its aspects and extend their repertoire.
FOLLOW-UP 1	Ask pairs of students to prepare dialogues expressing a particular mood for the next lesson. They say them in threes, taking body language, tone of voice, and intonation into account. The third student provides feedback. Help them when necessary. Make a tape recording and ask another group to try and recognize the mood from the voice only.
FOLLOW-UP 2	Get your learners to relax very deeply (see the Variation of 1.1). Ask them to concentrate on the intonation and tone of voice only. Then ask them to use the intonation and tone in an activity where they can express whatever they like.

2.23 Show your attitude/meaning

LEVEL	**Elementary and above**
TIME	**10 minutes**
AIMS	**Warming up; developing mastery of intonation for particular purposes; internalizing intonation 'rules'**
MATERIALS	**Slips of paper with attitudes written on**
PREPARATION	Prepare slips of paper with words describing attitudes which can be conveyed with the help of intonation, for example: *sceptical, enthusiastic, bored, amused, questioning, official.*
PROCEDURE	1 Tell the students that they can draw lots for an attitude to adopt for the whole lesson. One student takes a slip of paper and reads the attitude out. Tell the class they are going to practise expressing that attitude.
	2 Ask the students to stand in a circle (or several circles if there are too many learners). Ask for a volunteer in each circle to step forward and make an 'English/American noise', conveying the attitude on the slip of paper with their body language and intonation. If you and the group are satisfied, imitate it and make other noises, still expressing the same attitude. If you are not satisfied, step forward and demonstrate.
	3 Other students choose slips of paper. All the students make appropriate noises. Then concentrate on the last attitude chosen.
	4 Ask half the students to use body language only, while the other half use only sound and intonation.

5 When you are satisfied that the group is doing this reasonably well, say a word with the same attitude. The group follows.

6 When you are satisfied with this, say a short sentence for your students to imitate.

7 Tell your students to adopt the same attitude and intonation for the rest of the lesson.

8 Continue the lesson with a role play or discussion which fits the attitude adopted.

FOLLOW-UP

In further lessons, do similar activities to help distinguish, for example, the difference between a 'yes/no' question and an open question.

COMMENTS

This kind of preparation is extremely valuable before a role play or drama activity. For instance, 'subdued' and 'official' attitudes could be practised before playing a sketch involving a traffic offender and a traffic warden, for example. See *Role Play* (Porter-Ladousse 1987) and *Drama* (Wessels 1987) in this series for ideas. See also 2.24, 'Not the news'.

2.24 Not the news

LEVEL

Intermediate and above

TIME

30–60 minutes (can include homework)

AIMS

Internalizing basic intonation; practising intonation in certain situations and roles and going beyond them

MATERIALS

An audio or video recording of the news, and a transcript of a passage

PREPARATION

Record a recent news bulletin in English. Choose a passage about two minutes long at the level of your students. Make a transcript of part of it.

PROCEDURE

1 Play the news broadcast. The students listen and make notes on the content. Play it again, but this time ask your students to listen attentively to find out how the structure, rhythm, and intonation serve the purpose of the newsreader. Discuss this with the class.

2 (Optional) Ask them to relax and to listen, preferably with their eyes closed, moving their head and the upper part of their body to the rhythm and intonation of the passage. They open their eyes and go on moving as before, echoing the rhythm and intonation of the passage.

3 Hand out the transcripts. In pairs, the students practise being news announcers, keeping to the same text and rhythm.

4 (This can be done for homework.) Ask the students to prepare a local news bulletin, the news in their house or street, for example, keeping the same style and intonation. They read these to each other in pairs. Ask for volunteers to read theirs out to the class.

5 Ask your students to prepare and read out a second news bulletin, this time with a different style and intonation. They can, for example, sound flippant, subtly show they find the news uninteresting, adopt an ironical tone and intonation when reporting political news or a horrified attitude when reporting catastrophes, etc.

VARIATIONS

This activity gives scope for a lot of practice. You can use the same technique with other fairly ritualized situations, such as:

- announcements at airports and railway stations
- official receptions and parties
- police enquiries
- trials
- oral reports
- telephone enquiries
- presenting a recipe on television
- providing travel information (air, sea, road)
- a product demonstration (how a photocopying machine works, how to use a cashpoint, etc.).

COMMENTS

1 Advise students who find it hard to internalize the model to work on this at home. They should lie down comfortably, relax completely (as in 1.1B and Variation), and listen to a recording of English or to the radio. They should allow the sound of the language to penetrate them for about five minutes, concentrating on the intonation and rhythm only. They can then try to produce something similar.

2 Some kinds of ritual communication tend to require a certain style, rhythm, and intonation which are easy to recognize and fairly straightforward to get into. This provides a starting point for internalizing a basic framework and a point of reference for the learners to expand their register and become natural communicators.

2.25 Tales

LEVEL

Elementary and above

TIME

60 minutes

AIMS

Developing mastery of intonation through acting out stories

MATERIALS

The 'skeleton' of a tale, a short recording of music that fits the mood of the tale (optional), slips of paper

PREPARATION

1 Select a tale that suits your class's level of English. Conversations and exchanges between the characters must be introduced easily.

2 Prepare a 'skeleton' as in *Once Upon a Time* (Morgan and Rinvolucri 1983), suggesting where dialogues should appear. Here we use 'Rumpelstiltzkin' from *The Blue Fairy Book* (Lang 1975) as an example.

The letter [D] indicates that a dialogue can be inserted at that point, and [M] a monologue.

PROCEDURE

1 Tell the class they are going to listen to a tale and then act it out, improvising as they do so. Tell the story. Initially expand the story as much as possible, using mime and gesture and different intonations; for example, when the little man says 'no' several times. As you proceed, expand and act less. This gives your learners more opportunity for personal creation, instead of imitating you.

If your class is at intermediate or advanced level or experienced in this kind of activity, expand the story less and act as little as you can.

2 Put the class into groups of five. They prepare slips of paper with the names of the characters and each draw a slip. In 'Rumpelstiltzkin' there are five characters (father, daughter, king, Rumpelstiltzkin, messenger). If necessary, you can send out more messengers or the same student can play both the father and the messenger, as they never appear together.

3 Ask the students to sit comfortably and to close their eyes if they wish. Play the music softly and ask them to imagine their character going through the story. In a quiet, slow voice, tell them to picture themselves: their clothes, age, physical appearance. What time of the day and year is it? What are the surroundings like? What kind of character are they: fearful, optimistic? What is their mood on that particular day?

4 Describe one or two scenes from the story, very concisely, asking the class to picture the scene, smell the odours, feel the atmosphere, realize how they feel, and hear their voices. Stop for

Example

A miller, very beautiful daughter.

Father meets king—how? where? Describe father and king (physique and character, what kind of voice, mood, attitude?)

[D] Miller tells king his daughter can spin straw into gold. King wants girl to come and spin for him.

[D] Daughter with the king—what does he say? What does she feel?

[M] Daughter alone in tower, desperate, moans.

[D] Little man appears: will spin gold in exchange for her necklace. How the girl feels after the man's help.

[D] King happy in the morning—puts her in another room full of straw: spin into gold, or else!

[M] Girl more desperate.

[D] Little man—spins in exchange for her ring.

[D] King happy in the morning. Girl in larger room: more straw to spin or else! If yes, she will become queen.

[D] Little man again, but she must give him her first child.

[M] Daughter's thoughts as she agrees.

[D] King happy and marries her.

A year later a son is born. The little man comes back.

[D] 'Your son, or else'—'No'—offers lots of riches—little man wants living creature. Queen weeps. Little man gives her three days: if she can guess his name, she may keep child.

[D] Queen sends a messenger to collect names.

[D] Next day tells all the names she knows. 'No, that's not my name.' (How does the queen feel? And the little man?)

Next day the messenger finds more names.

[D] Little man comes back, listens to list but 'No'.

[D] The messenger: no new names, but in the wood a little house with a man singing and dancing:

> Today I brew, tomorrow I bake,
> And then the child away I'll take;
> For little knows my royal dame
> That Rumpelstiltzkin is my name!

Queen delighted.

[D] Little man comes, she says a few names, and then 'Rumpelstiltzkin'. (The queen's mood? Does she hide it?)

'The devil told you', he screamed, and stamped his right foot with such rage that he sank to his waist in the ground and tore himself into two.

5–10 seconds every time there is an element you want them to imagine. When you come to the end, wait, ask your class to picture a road from wherever they were in the story to the school, and to come back into the classroom, picture their group in their mind, and to open their eyes.

If you do not use music, allow the groups to build up the story together, brainstorming ideas. Tell them anything goes!

5 If necessary, hand out the story outline. The groups improvise, paying particular attention to the feelings of the characters by using gesture and intonation. Provide advice and help. Give them a quarter of an hour to do this.

6 Ask the groups to perform for each other. Each group should watch at least one other group perform.

VARIATION 1

Allow your students to choose their parts themselves sometimes.

VARIATION 2

Instead of preparing a complete tale yourself, offer a very general outline, for example: a castle, a magician, a dragon, a girl. In groups, the learners must then negotiate to create a tale they will act out.

VARIATION 3

Stories from comics and cartoons can also be used. Write the names of the characters on a slip of paper. Give a setting and the general attitude of each character, or ask the class to invent these. Then allow your students to improvise.

Example

> Thompson and Thomson (two accident-prone policemen in Tintin's adventures) have just arrested a skeleton. Improvise their conversation with the skeleton.

FOLLOW-UP

When your students are ready, they can play more 'realistic' role plays. Having involved themselves deeply in the characters of tales, they can join the games of real life with more ease.

COMMENTS

1 'The Three Little Pigs' and 'The Three Billy Goats Gruff' are very well suited for this. Andrew Wright's *Storytelling with Children* in this series also has a number of stories suitable for acting out.

2 Tales are excellent contexts for acquiring/practising intonation. They enable learners to take on any personality, and help to free them from the inhibitions which normally hamper the acquisition of intonation.

3 Approaching speech sounds

The activities in this chapter deal specifically with a number of sources of resistance to the speech sounds (phonemes) of English and help to develop awareness of how individual learners differentiate them. Learners are encouraged to approach the sounds of English by personalizing them and using as many aspects as possible of their ability to perceive. The activities are relevant irrespective of the learners' mother tongue; when nationalities are mentioned, they are just given as examples.

Learners are first shown how to listen to English speech sounds with new ears and to develop their inner feeling of what English sounds are like (3.1 and 3.2). They are encouraged to discuss their personal impressions of the phonemes of English (3.3).

They are also asked to approach the differences between sounds in a variety of ways, involving as many senses as possible, and appealing to their feelings and imagination (3.4–3.12).

Many of the activities give the learners opportunities to approach the actual production of sounds in ways that are playful, but which aim at achieving specific improvements (3.10–3.16).

Activities 3.4 (follow-up 1), 3.6 (follow-up 3), 3.13 and 3.17 show some enjoyable ways to approach the links between spelling and pronunciation.

Many of the activities in this chapter (3.2, follow-up 2; 3.8–3.10; 3.13; 3.17; 3.18) also try to generate a personal relationship with the sounds of the language by activating the learners' sense of beauty.

3.1 Re-invent English

LEVEL	All
TIME	**20–25 minutes**
AIMS	**Helping students to gradually sound more British/ American, etc.**
MATERIALS	**A short audio or video recording (about 3 minutes) of English speakers your learners can identify with**
PROCEDURE	1 Play the audio or video recording. Then ask your class to sit

comfortably with their eyes closed, and play it again. The class just listen. If you like, you can do 1.1B and Variation here.

2 They keep their eyes closed. In a calm and clear voice, ask them to imagine a situation where they hear English, for example, in films, on TV, or during their holidays. Ask them to imagine they are one of the people in the tape or video and to imagine *they themselves* are speaking. Stop talking for about thirty seconds or until you sense you should move on.

3 Tell the class to open their eyes, get into twos or threes, and pretend to 'speak' in 'English'. They are not expected to speak actual English, but to try to make a succession of English-sounding noises. It may help if they imagine they are parrots or apes imitating English or American speakers.

4 In groups of four, the students discuss what sounds they consider to be typically English (or American). Help them out with words they may need to give examples.

5 A representative from each group reports to the class. Write the sounds on the board, using phonemic script if your students are familiar with it, or else some form of spelling your students can easily associate with the pronunciation. Whenever the class agree on a sound, allow them to practise it.

6 Ask the groups to make up fake English words with the sounds and to compose a short 'speech' of 15–30 seconds. *They must first decide on the mood of the speech* (see chapter 2). They practise in their groups and decide who is going to perform for the group.

7 A representative from each group 'speaks' to the class. Everybody votes to decide who has made the most 'English' speech.

FOLLOW-UP 1

Ask your students to record on to cassettes fake English speeches. They can exchange the cassettes and later tell each other how good they think the speeches are.

FOLLOW-UP 2

In later lessons encourage volunteers to come and deliver an 'English' speech at the beginning of a lesson (it is an excellent warmer). You can give a topic: advertising a product in 'fake English' often works well. Encourage the use of gestures and body language to accompany their speeches, but they should not use sign language.

COMMENTS

1 This activity activates students' intuitive feelings of what English sounds like. It helps them to come to terms with sounding British/American, etc., and helps them discover what it takes.

2 If your learners do this activity at intervals you will notice how their awareness and mastery of English phonemes develops. This is also a good warmer and helps to overcome inhibitions.

Acknowledgements

This idea came to me from observing Jonathan, aged six, and from seeing Charlie Chaplin speaking fake German in *The Great Dictator*.

3.2 The most English sounds

LEVEL

All except complete beginners

TIME

15 minutes

AIMS

Developing awareness of the quality and specificity of English phonemes

PROCEDURE

This activity helps learners to realize that their awareness of English speech sounds is very personal. Do it in the students' mother tongue at beginner and elementary level.

1 Set the atmosphere by talking about your perception of English (or, if you are a native speaker, about your perception of the students' mother tongue). Tell them, for example, that in British English, you have always found /əʊ/ as in 'Oh, no!' very English, because you feel it is a sound with a 'distinctively English quality'. For American English you might take the final /r/ as in 'center' or 'manager' as an example. Also make it clear that this is a very personal feeling, and that there are no 'right' or 'wrong' perceptions.

2 Ask your students to write down words that contain the sounds they find most strikingly English (or American, etc.). The first time just ask them for one sound each; in later lessons ask for three to five.

3 Ask your students to compare their lists in pairs, and to explain why they find the sounds they have selected particularly characteristic.

4 Now ask your students to write down if they would like to be as English (or American, etc.) as their chosen sounds and why. The sounds chosen by the students reflect what they feel is 'Englishness/Americanness' in speech sounds. They may want to identify with this or not.

5 Allow them to discuss this in groups of four. It is a good idea for you to collect the lists as this can give you information to guide you in future work in class.

FOLLOW-UP

It is worth doing this activity several times at intervals to allow students to recognize their progress. You can also ask them to say which sounds they find 'most beautiful', 'most amusing', or 'most interesting'. Follow this activity with 3.18, 'Sound poetry'.

3.3 The easiest/most difficult sound(s)

LEVEL	**Not complete beginners**
TIME	**10–15 minutes**
AIMS	**Discovering that 'easiness' and 'difficulty' are relative**
MATERIALS	**A list of simple words your students know**

PREPARATION

Prepare your list of words on a large sheet of paper, on the board, or on an OHP transparency.

PROCEDURE

1 Begin by expressing your personal feelings about how easy you think the sounds of English are. Give examples, including sounds a number of your learners have problems with. Elicit reactions from the class and accept all of them.

2 Express surprise at the variety of responses, and suggest they ought to make an inventory of the easiest sounds in English. Show the class your list of words with examples of sounds. Pronounce the words yourself and ask your students to provide more words with sounds they would like to include.

3 Put the students in groups of about four, and give them at least five minutes to discuss which they think are the easiest sounds. They can include sounds which are not on the list. Provide help if necessary.

4 The students change groups and discuss again.

5 Ask each group to tell you which sounds they find easiest. Write them on the board in simple words. If anyone disagrees with any of the sounds suggested, allow the group to explain why they find them easy.

6 Encourage your students to make a list of easy sounds, or to write them down in their personal study diary.

FOLLOW-UP 1

Your students can prepare an advertisement for their favourite sound and present it to other learners or make a poster display.

FOLLOW-UP 2

Do this again after about a month, and ask your students to compare the two lists. Do the same for the 'most difficult' sounds of English, about two weeks later, and take note of the results to organize future work in class.

VARIATION

With young learners who cannot write yet, make drawings of concrete things or of actions: *a duck, dog, cat, bed, run, sleep,* etc. instead of using a list of words. For the group work, hand out pieces of paper for the pupils to draw on.

COMMENTS

This activity helps students to realize that what they find easy or difficult is not necessarily due to inherent difficulty. Discussion with other learners often helps to overcome problems, as other students may have a different opinion and another way of looking at the speech sounds.

3.4 Sounds and senses

LEVEL	**Elementary and above**
TIME	**10 minutes**
AIMS	**Associating sounds with other senses in order to distinguish them better**
MATERIALS	**For follow-up: pencils or felt-tipped markers of different colours**

PREPARATION Choose a vowel sound or diphthong your students do not find easy to pronounce. If they tend to confuse two sounds, choose those two and make a list of simple words with the sounds. For example: /aʊ/ (cow) and /əʊ/ (snow), /iː/ (read) and /ɪ/ (sit), /e/ (bed) and /æ/ (man).

PROCEDURE 1 Ask your students to sit comfortably and to close their eyes.

2 Tell them you are going to pronounce a sound several times, and that they should imagine a colour when they hear it.

3 Pronounce the sound in different ways, with 5 seconds' silence between each: whisper, shout, whine, repeat it rhythmically a couple of times, and prolong it.

4 Ask your class to write down the name of the colour they associate with the sound, and if possible the reason why they feel it has a link with that colour. Ask very young learners to use a coloured pencil.

5 If you are trying to help your students distinguish two sounds, do the same with the second one.

6 Put your learners in a circle and ask them to visualize the colour for the sound first, and then to say simple words containing the sound after you.

7 Now they can take the initiative, pronouncing words while still visualizing the colour they associate with the sound.

VARIATION This activity can also be done with consonants your learners find difficult to distinguish. It works best with fricatives, for example /s/ and /z/, /f/ and /v/, /dʒ/ (join) and /tʃ/ (change).

FOLLOW-UP 1 Students write lists of words containing the sounds, writing the sounds in the colour they saw during the activity. Then they write poems (see 3.18) using the colours they saw, making pleasant colour combinations. They can also decorate a house using speech sound colours: what room or even part of a room would they paint with particular sounds?

FOLLOW-UP 2

1 Ask your students to associate sounds with tastes and textures. Begin with sounds they can distinguish easily, such as /ʃ/ in 'shut' and /p/ in 'part', then choose sounds they find more difficult to distinguish. Ask the class to choose between two tastes, for example: savoury or sweet, plain or spicy, crunchy or soft, juicy or dry, raw or cooked, food for every day or special occasions.

2 Tell your students to pronounce words with the sounds to themselves about 10 times and to decide how they taste.

3 Ask them to make up a 'sound menu' for breakfast, lunch, tea, dinner, and supper, or to compose recipes for different days of the week.

Examples

Here are some examples of colour and taste associations made by learners who were asked to distinguish /e/ and /æ/:

/e/: yellow/grapefruit, red/melon, light blue/chocolate, grey/salt, white/apple, yellow/sweet, yellow/blue/salty

/æ/: brown/beer, black/onion, black/lemon, black/potatoes with butter, blue/dry, black/water melon, red/ice-cream.

3.5 Feeling the vowels

'Our body is the instrument our thoughts use in order to speak.'

Tomatis 1963: 147

LEVEL

All

TIME

5 minutes

AIMS

Improving pronunciation by associating sounds with parts of the body

PROCEDURE

1 If you have a teenage or adult class, give them the quotation above and ask them to discuss it.

2 Tell them that different vowel sounds cause different parts of the body to vibrate.

3 Ask them to produce sounds (see below) and to feel where the vibration is. They put both hands on the parts of their body that you indicate. Ask them to say where they feel the sound. They

will also notice that the vibrations made by different sounds are of different quality.

/i:/ as in 'sea': neck (throat and nape)
/e/ as in 'set': collar bone and upper ribs
/æ/ as in 'cat': as above plus some lower ribs; a different vibration
/ɑ:/ as in 'dark': more vibration, lower in the ribs and diaphragm
/ɔ:/ as in 'door': causes a different vibration again
and so on for /ʊ/, /u:/, and /ɜ:/.

4 Encourage your learners to experiment by feeling different parts of the neck and rib-cage. They will find that the higher the sound, the higher the part of their bodies that vibrates. The highest sounds also cause a vibration in the skull.

5 Ask the students to sit in pairs and produce the same sounds together. They feel the sounds in their own bodies and exchange their impressions.

FOLLOW-UP 1

1 Where culturally acceptable, use this for peer correction. Make pairs with one student who can pronounce the sound well and one who does not. They put one hand on their partner and the other on themselves and try to feel the same vibration in themselves as in their partner.

2 Students who need to improve put both their hands on their own rib-cage. This time their partners give feedback based on what they can hear.

FOLLOW-UP 2

Use this technique to help learners distinguish between sounds which they believe are the same in their mother tongue as in English.

Acknowledgements

This activity is derived from Aucher 1977.

3.6 What sound can you make?

LEVEL

All

TIME

15 minutes

AIMS

Learning how sounds are produced

PREPARATION

Find out what simple instructions you need to give for particular sounds (see Further Reading: Dalton and Seidlhofer 1994, Roach 1986, Avery and Ehrlich 1992).

PROCEDURE

1 Get your students to relax and breathe in English (see 1.1B and C).

2 Choose sounds that your learners need to practise. Ask them to use their organs of speech in certain ways, and to say what sounds they can produce (see the examples below).

3 Ask the learners to think of, then say, words with the chosen sound, for example, 'hope', 'heap', 'hip', 'house' for /h/. They need to be physically aware of the language and feel the sounds and words taking shape in them as they breathe.

4 Encourage the students to play at 'talking' in pairs, using the sounds they have discovered with intonation and body language. A convincing-sounding 'conversation' can be conducted in this way with just a few sounds.

EXAMPLES

1 Learners discover that by breathing out they can produce /h/.

2 Get your learners to discover what sound is produced by breathing out, with the lower lip lightly touching the upper teeth (/f/). Add voicing (they can feel it with their hands on their throats) and they get /v/.

3 Breathing with the tongue nearly (but not quite) touching the back of the teeth produces /s/; add voicing for /z/.

4 For plosives, ask your learners what sounds they produce when they put different parts of their mouth together, then release their breath in different ways (e.g. voiced or unvoiced).

3.7 Sounds and movements

LEVEL

All

TIME

5 minutes

AIMS

Improving pronunciation by associating sounds with movements

PREPARATION

Choose the sound(s) you wish to work on and think of movements the class can make which fit the sound(s). The suggestions below are merely meant to give you ideas, and by no means include all sounds of English. Pronounce the sound(s) with your learners and invent suitable gestures with them.

EXAMPLES

Sounds with short movements:
short vowels /ɪ/, /e/, /æ/, /ʌ/ as in 'shut', /ɒ/ as in 'dot', /ʊ/, /ə/ as in 'again': use short movements with a hand or finger to mirror the movement of the tongue. Front and back vowels can be contrasted with arm movements.
voiceless plosives /p/, /t/, /k/: short, sudden movements such as clapping.

Sounds with longer movements:

voiced plosives /b/, /d/, /g/: movements such as folding the arms with fists clenched as the learners close their mouths; as the sound is released they gently unfold their arms and unclench their fists to leave the arms outstretched and hands open.

nasals /m/, /n/, /ŋ/, as well as /l/: a longer movement, e.g. starting with arms half-bent with the hands at shoulder height; as the learners close their mouths, they clench their hands and tighten their arm muscles. As the sound is released they relax their muscles.

unvoiced fricatives and affricates /f/, /θ/ as in 'thick', /s/, /ʃ/ as in 'ship', /tʃ/ as in 'choose': longer movements such as pushing outward with the hands.

long vowels /iː/, /ɑː/, /ɔː/ as in 'pour', /uː/ as in 'pool', /ɜː/ as in 'world', and diphthongs /əʊ/, /aɪ/, etc.: use larger hand or arm movements, or even stand up or sit down.

Sounds with even longer movements:

voiced fricatives and affricates /v/, /z/, /ð/ as in 'those', /ʒ/ as in 'measure', /dʒ/ as in 'journey', plus affricates and /w/.

In this activity /h/, /j/, and /r/ are best practised with a vowel sound after them.

PROCEDURE	1 Tell your students what sound(s) they are going to practise. Ask them to list words they know with those sounds in.

2 Pronounce the sounds on their own first and ask the class to say them after you. Ask them to accompany the sound with a gesture (see above).

3 Pair off the learners; if some are better at these sounds they can act as models for less proficient partners.

4 Finally, get the learners to do this while pronouncing whole words.

FOLLOW-UP

Learners can also practise recognizing pairs of sounds or sound clusters they find hard to distinguish.

1 Choose two sounds and movements to go with them.

2 Pair off the students. One says a sound and the other makes what they think is the appropriate movement.

You can gradually increase the number of sounds to a maximum of five.

VARIATION

Young learners can play at actually being speech sounds and act out a word.

COMMENTS

This is a good warmer at the beginning of a lesson, especially if you let learners decide on the sounds and movements.

Acknowledgements

The starting point for this activity comes from Dufeu 1992.

3.8 Sound metaphors and similes

LEVEL

All except beginners

TIME

20 minutes

AIMS

Distinguishing speech sounds through associations with other sounds and personal impressions

PROCEDURE

1 Talk with your students about how similar speech sounds are to other sounds in our environment. Give a 'crazy' example such as '/i:/ always makes me think of a horse laughing'.

2 Ask your students to sit comfortably, close their eyes, and relax (see 1.1B). Ask them to think of what the sound they hear is like: 'This is a …', or 'this is like a …'.

3 Produce a speech sound that they have problems with, and play with it by moving your voice up and down and prolonging

the sound. If you have chosen a plosive, repeat it several times. You may need to add a schwa (the first sound in 'again' /ə/) to make some consonants more audible.

4 The students write down their impressions of the sound and discuss them in groups. Help them with any vocabulary they may need to express what they want to say.

5 If you like, do the same with a sound that some may confuse with the first one, for example, /z/ and /ð/, and to compare their ideas.

Some examples of associations made by learners:
/aʊ/ is a cat mewing
/h/ is a leaf carried away by a light breeze
/p/ is like a cork popping
/z/ is like a lawn-mower on a beautiful summer day
/s/ is like steam escaping from a boiling kettle
/ʒ/ is the sound of a bee buzzing from flower to flower, an ultra-light aeroplane on a summer day.

VARIATION

Ask the students to associate the sounds with animals and people they know.

3.9 The happiest sound

LEVEL

All except complete beginners

TIME

30 minutes plus homework

AIMS

Distinguishing sounds

PREPARATION

Prepare a hand-out based on the one below, or ask the questions orally.

SAMPLE HAND-OUT

1 _____	is the highest sound in English.
2 _____	is the lowest sound in English.
3 _____	is the softest sound in English.
4 _____	is the loudest sound in English.
5 _____	is the saddest sound in English.
6 _____	is the happiest sound in English.

Photocopiable © Oxford University Press

You could also ask which sound is the funniest, most aggressive, interesting, boring, energetic, female, childish, 'catlike', 'birdlike', etc.

PROCEDURE

1 Ask your students to talk about everyday sounds they like or do not like: 'I hate the sound of a nail on a window pane, it makes me shiver' or 'I love the sound of a brook in a forest'.

2 Now turn to language. Give out the hand-out or ask your questions. The learners write their answers and compare them in pairs, changing partners a couple of times.

3 At home, your students find words with the sound that contradict and fit the adjective they have associated with the sounds. Next lesson ask them to compare their lists in pairs.

4 Later, choose (or allow your learners to choose) two sounds they would like to contrast, for example, /i:/ and /ɪ/. Ask them to find adjectives that fit the sounds, or provide a list for them to choose from. Ask them to explain their choices in pairs: 'It's an aggressive vowel like a ...', 'It makes me think of ...'.

VARIATION

Ask your students to identify with a sound from a limited list. Then ask them to mill around trying to look like the sound they have chosen, miming the 'character' of the sound. Stop them after one minute, and ask them to find a partner. The partner tries to guess which sound they have chosen. They talk about it. This works particularly well with young learners.

3.10 Draw the sound

LEVEL

All

TIME

5–10 minutes

AIMS

Distinguishing phonemes by drawing them

MATERIALS

Pens/pencils and paper

PREPARATION

Choose a couple of sounds your students need practice in distinguishing.

PROCEDURE

1 Tell your learners you would like them to associate speech sounds with drawings (any kind will do). Make it clear this has nothing to do with writing the sounds, and that all drawings are equally valid.

2 The learners should sit comfortably with a blank sheet of paper in front of them and a pen in their hands, ready to draw.

3 Ask your class to close their eyes and to relax, for example by breathing in and out, concentrating on the sound their breathing makes. Calmly tell them you are going to pronounce one of the sounds you have chosen; they should allow their hand to respond by drawing something. Say the sound a couple of times.

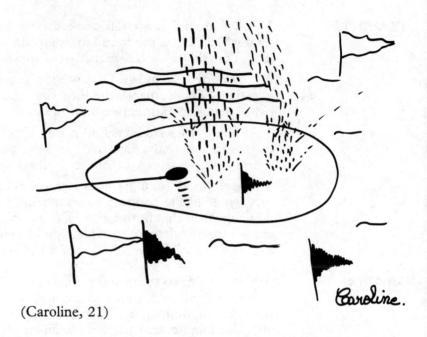

(Caroline, 21)

(Joseph, 20)

4 Ask them to do the same with the other sound on a clean sheet of paper.

5 Ask the learners to look at their drawings and to discuss them with a partner.

FOLLOW-UP 1

Ask your learners to design wallpaper or fabric using their drawings. What rooms of their house would they decorate with an /i:/ pattern? What kind of clothes or furniture would they make with the fabric? Or they could pretend to be hotel managers and decorate each room with a different sound—and then decide what kind of person they would put in each room.

FOLLOW-UP 2

Proceed as above with several sounds but ask your learners to draw them in one drawing. In pairs they read their drawings to each other, or try to 'read' what they see in their partner's drawing. Allow them to discuss this. See the examples on page 94.

FOLLOW-UP 3

If you have also associated sound with colours (see 3.4), ask your students to 'discover' the sounds in a painting, or in a photograph of a landscape.

3.11 Musical sounds

LEVEL

All

TIME

5–10 minutes

AIMS

Improving the pronunciation of speech sounds through rhythm, singing, and movement

MATERIALS

Short recordings of suitable music

PREPARATION

Decide which sounds you want to work on and choose a suitable piece of music two to three minutes long (see suggestions below). Prepare a recording, or if you play an instrument other than a wind instrument, you can play it yourself.

For voiceless plosive consonants /p/, /t/, /k/ and short vowels /ɪ/ (sit), /e/ (get), /æ/ (bat), /ʌ/ (cut), /ɒ/ (dock), /ʊ/ (cook), use a piece of music where the rhythmic element is more striking.

Flowing, melodic tunes work best with voiced plosives, the fricatives, and longer vowels /i:/ (deep), /ɑ:/ (dark), /ɔ:/ (door), /u:/ (cool). Slow tunes are useful for diphthongs, to enable your learners to gradually move from the onset position of the diphthong to the final position so that all the elements come out distinctly.

PROCEDURE

1 Tell your students that today you would like them to *sing* an English sound, which is a very natural activity, as speaking is musical.

2 Sing or say your chosen sound (short vowels and plosive voiceless consonants as a short burst, long vowels sung on a fairly high note). Encourage your students to sing with you. If you feel you are not a good singer, tell them so! This will help them overcome their own fears about their musical abilities. Remind them that the aim is to play with the sound so as to get used to it.

3 Play the music and sing the sound, singing it to the tune. Encourage the class to join in. For short vowels, voiceless plosive consonants, and the voiceless affricate /tʃ/ they sing when they feel the beat. For other sounds (longer vowels, voiced plosive consonants, the voiced affricate /dʒ/, fricative consonants, and diphthongs) they sing to the tune. Some will join in right away, others a bit later.

4 Now get your learners to walk to the music as well. They can tap their feet for short sounds and sing others, as before. If you wish you can add suitable hand movements as well (see 3.7).

FOLLOW-UP 1

When the class are happy singing both types of sounds, try putting them together. One half of the class follows the beat with one sound and gesture, while the other sings the tune with another sound and gesture.

FOLLOW-UP 2

When the class can all sing a vowel, put a consonant before it: /p/, /t/, and /h/ are particularly worth trying, as the students can practise the aspiration that goes with these consonants as well. They can then do the activity using short words containing the chosen sound.

FOLLOW-UP 3

Make a speech sound orchestra.

1 Play a recording of a number of musical instruments, asking the students to decide which instruments the speech sound sounds like. For example, /p/ as in 'put' may be the sound of a trumpet, /ʃ/ as in 'show' a percussion or a synthesizer sound, and /ʊ/ as in 'look' the sound produced by a flute or ocarina. Try this in groups.

2 Students choose their 'instruments' and sing as before.

Try this out yourself before doing it in class.

COMMENTS

It is best to associate vowels with a particular tune at first, using the same tune with each vowel all the time.

Suggested music

The following music has worked well with my students. Always try the music out yourself first, for perception can vary according to cultures. You should be able to find other suitable pieces in consultation with your learners.

A For voiceless plosive consonants, /ʧ/, glides /j/ and /w/, and short vowels

1 Paganini: Concerto no. 1, Op. 6 in D Major: 1st movement (beginning)

2 Dvořák: 'New World' Symphony: Beginning and other excerpts from the fourth movement (about two minutes). Excellent for plosive consonants and /ʧ/.

3 Kitaro: 'Silk Road': ask your students to say the sounds when they feel a beat in the music.

B For fricative consonants, voiced plosives, nasals, and /ʤ/ (direct your learners' attention to the melody!)

1 Mozart: Flute concerto no 1, K313, first movement

2 Paganini: Violin Concerto no 2 in E minor, Op. 7: 2nd movement, an excerpt from the main part.

3 New Age music such as Edward Christmas's 'Song of the Golden Lotus'.

C For longer vowels and diphthongs

Some music is better suited for open vowels and some for closed vowels—it is a question of pitch. Once you have found a piece that you think is suitable, try to sing one of the vowels along with it—you will soon feel which vowels go best with the tune.

1 Johann Strauss (younger): excerpts from the 'Blue Danube' waltz ('An der schönen blauen Donau'). This is well-suited to lower vowels, /ɑː/ in particular.

2 Lehár: aria from *The Merry Widow* 'Lippen schweigen, 's flüstern Geigen' ('Lips are silent, violins whisper')—orchestral section (/iː/, /uː/, /ɔː/ as in 'pour')

3 The Beatles: 'Yesterday'. Best for /ɑː/ and /uː/, but can also be used for /əʊ/ as in 'throw', if the second element is suitably lengthened.

4 Gregorian chants, where culturally acceptable, can be excellent for practising vowels and diphthongs.

Acknowledgements

An article by Krnic and Wambach (1989) has helped me to find ways to generalize this approach to nearly all the sounds of the English language.

3.12 Echoes

LEVEL

All

TIME

5 minutes

AIMS

Practising any vowel sound or diphthong, warming up

PREPARATION

Choose a vowel or diphthong you would like your students to work on. Think of some simple words, preferably one-syllable words, containing the vowel or diphthong.

PROCEDURE

1 Put the students in a circle, and make a vowel-like sound. It does not have to be a phoneme of any language you or your students know.

2 Ask the class to imitate you.

3 Encourage the students to play with the sound by making it longer, saying it on a higher or lower pitch, or by whispering it, shouting it, expressing sorrow, joy, enthusiasm, despair, etc. (in this way playing with intonation as well). The best way to get them to do this is by contributing a variation of the sound yourself now and then.

4 Take over, but this time pronounce an English vowel and repeat steps 1–3.

5 Choose a word, preferably a one-syllable word which has the vowel in it, and continue as before. In later lessons you can do the same with other vowels or diphthongs.

FOLLOW-UP

For further practise in pronouncing vowels and diphthongs, get your learners to 'tune' a vowel or diphthong.

1 Say a sound and hold it as long as you can. Signal to a student to do the same as you, then another, until all the students have held the sound as long as they can. (If the class is large, divide it into groups of about twelve.)

2 Next do this with words, and later with two-syllable words or utterances such as 'Oh no!', 'pay day', or 'I buy'.

3.13 Dy spk Nglsh?

LEVEL

All learners who can read and write English

TIME

5–10 minutes

AIMS

Developing the ability to pronounce clusters and weak forms correctly, and to reduce vowels in weakly stressed syllables

PROCEDURE	**1** Tell the class they are going to try to find to what extent vowels are necessary when speaking English. In groups of four, ask them to prepare a short dialogue from which they should remove all the vowels. Monitor this carefully, as they may forget the semi-vowels (/j/, /w/) and include sounds corresponding to letters that are not pronounced (the 'r' after vowels in British English for example).

Example

Dy spk Nglsh? (Do you speak English?)
Lttl, cn hlp y? (A little, can I help you?)
Whs th pst ffc? (Where's the post office?)
Tn rt ft th trfc lts, ts th scnd strt n th lft. (Turn right after the traffic lights, it's the second street on the left.)

2 The students try to say this. Then ask them to add as few vowels as possible until it becomes understandable. In the case of the dialogue above, a good result would be:

Dy speak English?
A littl, cn I help y?
Where's th post office?
Turn right after th traffc lights, its th secnd street n th left.

FOLLOW-UP 1	In later activities, introduce rhythm and intonation as well.
FOLLOW-UP 2	When the learners practise this again in later lessons, provide variety by asking them to make up amusing dialogues and say them as if they were comic characters such as Harold Lloyd, Laurel and Hardy, Benny Hill, Thomson and Thompson, etc.
COMMENTS	This shows where vowels can be reduced to make words sound more English, by using weak forms.

3.14 Vowel/consonant songs

LEVEL	**All**
TIME	**5–10 minutes the first time, a couple of minutes in later lessons**
AIMS	**Practising speech sounds and associating them with spellings**
MATERIALS	**A version of a song, with each syllable replaced with a single vowel sound**
PREPARATION	Choose a simple song your students know well, such as 'Frère Jacques'. Prepare a version of the song with each syllable

replaced by a vowel sound. Use a possible spelling of the sound or the phonemic symbol.

Example

phonemic symbol	*'a' as in 'ape'*
/eɪ eɪ eɪ eɪ, eɪ eɪ eɪ eɪ,	a a a a, a a a a
eɪ eɪ eɪ, eɪ eɪ eɪ	a a a, a a a
eɪ eɪ eɪ eɪ eɪ eɪ	a a a a a a
eɪ eɪ eɪ eɪ eɪ eɪ	a a a a a a
eɪ eɪ eɪ, eɪ eɪ eɪ/	a a a, a a a

Try this out before you use it in class.

PROCEDURE

1 Encourage your class to sing the song in any language, just to warm them up and give them confidence.

2 Now they are going to rewrite the song. First they write it down. Then ask them, individually, to replace each syllable with the phonemic symbol or the spelling you have chosen for your vowel sound. (This is also a simple exercise in syllable counting.) If you have chosen the spelling, do not pronounce the sound, but write it on the board. Ask your students how they would pronounce it. They will probably come up with several possibilities. Tell them which pronunciation you would like to concentrate on—for example, 'a' as in 'ape' rather than as in 'car'.

3 Ask your students to compare their versions with each other, and then show them your prepared version.

4 Sing the new 'song' with your students, gently encouraging those who feel embarrassed, until everyone is singing it. You may like to ask some students who appear very uninhibited to come and sing alone or as a choir in front of the class. It is a good idea to invite the class to accompany them by clapping the rhythm.

FOLLOW-UPS

The follow-ups are crucial because this activity is particularly effective when practised fairly regularly over a longer period, introducing variations every time. With beginners, do it whenever a new spelling of a phoneme is encountered.

FOLLOW-UP 1

Repeat the activity with other vowel sounds, then replace the phonemic symbol or first spelling with others.

1 First, mix two spellings. Ask your students to find one-syllable words in which the two spellings are used. Use several words with the same spelling of the sound:

    ay ay ei ei, ay ay ei ei
    day may vein rein …

2 Expand the range of spellings used, for example, replace 'a' with 'ai', 'ay', 'ei', 'ey', 'ea' (as in 'great') or 'au' (as in 'gauge'):

    ape rain great day …

FOLLOW-UP 2

The students combine words in such a way that meaningful, amusing, or memorable associations are produced:

> May day May day
> space ray space ray
> eight grey apes sleighed
> eight state freight trains, weigh great pay weights

FOLLOW-UP 3

Add consonant sounds as an additional challenge, e.g.:

> wail whale sail sale
> cake cape cage case

FOLLOW-UP 4

Mix different vowel sounds, e.g.:

> /eɪ aɪ eɪ aɪ, eɪ aɪ eɪ aɪ/
> heigh high eight height …
> /aɪ aɪ eɪ ɔɪ/
> bye bye bay boy

FOLLOW-UP 5

To distinguish different pronunciations of the same letter in different environments you can make up 'songs' like this one for /æ/ and /eɪ/, which can both be represented by the letter 'a'.

> cat Kate pal pale …

Some suggested tunes

Frère Jacques
Brahms: Wiegenlied (Lullaby)
Baa baa, black sheep
The animals came in two by two

COMMENTS

This activity simulates the skills a baby uses when playing with the sounds of the language as it is learning to speak.

3.15 Mirror on the wall

LEVEL

All

TIME

5–10 minutes

AIMS

Learning to use the lips and facial muscles to pronounce English better

PROCEDURE

1 Tell your students they are going to be actors and actresses preparing for a performance, in order to develop a 'beautiful English face' as they try to pronounce a particular sound or word. They will help each other by being each other's mirror, reflecting their partner's facial expressions.

2 Working in pairs, one student is the mirror, and the other an actor/actress practising. Allow them to choose which they want to be.

3 Ask them all to look very carefully at you. Pronounce a series of short words (up to five) beginning with the sound, and change your mood every time. If this is the first time, keep it simple: choose one word only and say it in as many moods as you can think of, expressing the moods with your tone of voice as well as your face. Also vary the pitch.

Examples

holidays: hopeful, happy, serene, sleepy, sorry—because they are finished …
wood: wistful, nostalgic, admiring, surprised, relaxed, happy, worried …

5 Now ask the actors and actress to say the word in front of their 'mirror', expressing as many moods as they can. The mirrors reflect their faces accurately, but are silent. Encourage the actors and actresses to go on trying until they like the expression reflected by their mirror and feel it looks as it should for the word or words practised.

6 They change mirrors a couple of times. Monitor carefully to see who has problems, so that you can help out or work more on the sounds later.

7 The learners discuss the activity: how it felt, what it takes to do it well, etc. Make sure everyone becomes an actor or actress at some stage.

FOLLOW-UP

In further lessons, choose words with the sound in other positions, for example: /w/ in 'way', 'away', 'awake'. Expand to two or more sounds or words which contrast sounds and facial movements, for example, 'west' and 'vest'; 'bid' and 'bad'; 'or', 'oh', and 'our'.

Activity 3.16, 'Silent dictation', is a logical sequel to this.

VARIATION 1

Organize a contest. Ask the learners who has the best 'English face' as they pronounce the words. This should be lively and not taken too seriously.

VARIATION 2

Start with the classic fairy tale *Snow White and the Seven Dwarfs* (Grimm). Concentrate on the passage where the queen looks in her mirror and asks 'Mirror, mirror on the wall, who is the fairest in all the land?' and tell your class they are going to be princes, princesses, or mirrors. The mirrors say who has the 'fairest English face' (i.e. the most convincing) in the land. If necessary, show the learners that there can be more than one way of being good-looking or 'fair'.

VARIATION 3

To warm up students and encourage them to use their facial muscles for sounds such as /əʊ/ as in 'show', /aʊ/ as in 'now', /w/, /θ/ as in 'thick', and /ð/ as in 'these', ask them to imagine that they are very intelligent chimpanzees trying to imitate human speech.

3.16 Silent dictation

LEVEL

All

TIME

5–10 minutes

AIMS

Acquiring the correct pronunciation of English sounds by becoming aware of the lip positions and movements

PREPARATION

Prepare a list of words, short sentences, or phrases containing sounds you wish to improve, and number them. Choose two sounds where the contrast in the articulation is clearly visible, for example:

toe–tea (shape of lips)
nought–not (lip rounding)
pet–bet (the first is more aspirated)
now–nor (the mouth and lip movements are different)
bug–buck (the length and release are different)
thick–sick (tongue showing in first word).

For very young learners use words referring to something you can draw ('bag' and 'bug' for example) and use a colour code instead of numbering.

PROCEDURE

1 Write the words or phrases on the board or hand them out, and go through them. Draw the students' attention to your face as you pronounce them.

Explain that you are going to give them a silent dictation, and that they will have to recognize which word or sentence you are saying just by looking at you. Make sure all the learners can see you clearly.

Give an example:

    Have you seen the men? (1)
    Have you seen the man? (2)

Dictate silently: move your face and lips as if you were pronouncing.

2 The students write down the number of the sentence or the sentence itself.

3 Check their answers. Ask students who got it right to explain to the rest of the class what they noticed when you pronounced different sounds.

4 Try again with the other words or sentences. When most students appear to have got it right, move on to the next step.

5 Ask your students to prepare a short silent dictation in writing. Provide help if needed.

6 In pairs, they dictate their silent texts to each other.

7 They check their answers, correcting each other's performance.

8 They try again with another partner. The degree of accuracy in their recognition is an assessment of both the quality of the production and the ability to recognize.

FOLLOW-UP

Gradually develop your students' ability to lip-read sounds and to articulate well by giving them silent dictations with more and more different sounds.

This activity is best done after 3.15, 'Mirror on the wall'.

3.17 Whispers

LEVEL

All

TIME

10–15 minutes

AIMS

Distinguishing and articulating voiced and voiceless consonants in word endings

MATERIALS

Record cards

PREPARATION

Prepare a list of words with voiced or voiceless consonants at the end, such as bat, stop, dog. Write one word on each record card. Prepare enough for at least one card per student (they can help you to do this).

PROCEDURE

1 Ask your students to put a hand on their throat while they have a short conversation with a partner.

2 Tell them to repeat the conversation in a whisper. Ask for feedback: they should tell you they can feel nothing with their hand when they whisper.

3 Ask your learners to get up and mill around. Say alternatively voiced and voiceless consonants, putting a vowel in front of them (for example, /æk/ as in 'back', /ed/ as in 'said') both whispering and saying them aloud. The learners repeat them to each other in whispers.

In whispering part of the difference between the voiced and the voiceless sounds is lost, so they will have to 'pronounce' the voiced sounds very emphatically and take more time over them than the voiced ones. As an added bonus they will lengthen the vowel sounds preceding them. The voiceless consonants will also be released more strongly.

4 The learners return to their seats. Ask them if they had more problems with some sounds than with others. They should notice that there are consonants that are clear when whispered and others which are less so. Explain this difference and discuss how they can try to differentiate them.

5 As in Step 2, but feed in *words* this time: *bad, dog, robbed, stopped, played, weighed,* etc. Make sure they pay proper attention to the voiced endings.

6 Hand out the cards you have prepared and ask the learners, in pairs, to whisper their words to their partners, who must try to recognize the words.

7 Then the students pronounce the words normally, making sure they have the same feeling when they pronounce the voiced sounds (the sounds that are difficult to whisper) as when they were whispering. The others in the group must listen with their eyes closed and provide feedback. Whenever they are not satisfied they can hear the sounds properly, they ask the speaker to whisper first and then to say it normally.

FOLLOW-UP

For speakers of languages such as Thai, Chinese, and Vietnamese who tend to drop some end-consonants altogether, or do not release them, prepare lists of words ending in voiced and voiceless consonants, for example, foot–food, back–bag, lap–lab. Tell them to proceed as in Steps 2–4 above. Discuss with them how easy/difficult it is for them to recognize the words when they are whispered. Ask them to say the words normally, trying to make them clear.

COMMENTS

1 This activity is very useful for dealing with endings. Some speakers do not release the endings at all, while others add a schwa and a syllable.

2 The follow-up to activity 3.7, 'Sounds and movements', also improves pronunciation of these sounds.

3.18 Sound poetry

LEVEL

Elementary and above

TIME

About 20 minutes in one lesson, plus homework and more time in another lesson

AIMS

Playing aesthetically with speech sounds, pitch, and rhythm

| MATERIALS | **Optional: a recording of modern, concrete, or minimalist music** |

PREPARATION

If you wish, choose music to trigger your students' imagination. Recordings of concrete music are particularly appropriate, for example, Varèse's 'Poème électronique'. Other suitable pieces are Varèse's 'Déserts' (bars 225–263), or music by John Cage, Ligeti, Frank Martin, or Peter Michael Hamel. Japanese Zen music could also be used.

PROCEDURE

1 Proceed as in 3.2, 'The most English sounds' to get your students to select their *favourite* sounds in English, or simply ask them to suggest the most beautiful English sounds.

2 Ask them what everyday objects they think they could use to make music (e.g. spoons). Then suggest they could do the same with language sounds, composing poems by playing with the sounds they prefer, like musicians use the sound of their favourite objects to compose music. In this poetry it is not the words, but the beauty of the sounds and their arrangement in rhythmic patterns and changes in pitch which are important. This can be considered as 'pure' or 'sound' poetry.

You can get your meaning across more easily if you play a short excerpt of modern music as described above.

3 Ask your students for homework to prepare a short, personal sound poem, using isolated English language sounds or combinations, not forgetting rhythm and intonation, and to prepare to perform it in class next time (or if they prefer to record it for the next lesson). They can represent the sounds with either phonetic symbols or English spelling (see 3.14).

4 During the following lessons encourage your students to come and perform their poems or to play their recordings. Use this as a warmer or to relax the class when you sense their attention is lagging. Allow the class to respond. Encourage them to exchange their recorded sound poems with other students.

VARIATION 1

Ask your students to write their poem using specific sounds you would like them to practise.

VARIATION 2

The students compose a poem in groups and say it with different voices and sounds. Each student can specialize: for example, one says the plosives /b/, /p/, /k/, /g/, another some of the vowels, etc.

COMMENTS

Language sounds can be used for pure pleasure just to create attractive combinations. This helps learners to gradually get into the sound of English and is very effective for improving pronunciation at all levels.

3.19 Playing with sounds

Here are four examples of enjoyable activities based on speech sounds. You will be able to think of others.

Sound names

LEVEL	**Elementary and above**
PROCEDURE	Ask your learners to create for themselves names made up of their favourite sounds. They can choose the sounds to reflect their character or simply because they like them. Make sure combinations sound English. Allow them to use the name in class. Similarly, you can ask learners to create names for pets, products, etc.

Advertisements

LEVEL	**Lower-intermediate and above**
PROCEDURE	1 Give an example of an alliterative advertising slogan such as 'They've got to be great to be Guards' (a very old cigarette advertisement) or, if you do not approve of cigarette advertising, 'Wallow in Willow' (a margarine advert). Get your learners to say this and enjoy pronouncing it. Ask them why it is fun to say. Ask them what product they would advertise with it and to explain why. Accept all answers and do not tell them what it was for originally.

Other examples

'Beans means Heinz' (a brand of baked beans)
'This is the end of the line for litter' (London Underground campaign to put litter in litter bins)
'For mash get Smash' (instant mashed potato).

2 Ask the learners to make up a slogan like this for a product or an organization (for example, their school, their class, a sports team, a political party, a charity). These can be invented. Suggest they should also play with rhythm, pitch, voice quality, and intonation. This can be done for homework.

3 Next lesson, they present their advertisements and vote for the best one.

Onomatopoeia

LEVEL	**Lower-intermediate and above**
PROCEDURE	1 Give your class some examples of onomatopoeia in English: 'splash', 'bow-wow', 'atishoo!', 'bang bang!' If necessary, explain why they are onomatopoeic. Compare them with the corresponding renderings in their mother tongue(s).

2 Ask the students to make up watery sounds, metallic sounds, wooden sounds, etc. with English speech sounds.

3 Ask the learners to each prepare a spoken description using only onomatopoeia: for example, describe the noise of rain and the changes in the noise as the rain continues, or the noise of water running in a brook, the wind in the trees, a bicycle in the wind or rain, a motorcycle starting up and then going along the road, a lawn-mower, etc. Allow them to prepare this on a cassette at home.

4 Next lesson, play some cassettes and ask the learners to recognize what the other learners have tried to render. Then ask them what English speech sounds they can recognize. They discuss this with the 'composers'.

Sound tales

LEVEL

Intermediate

PROCEDURE

Ask your learners to invent a tale or story with words that include certain sounds, for example, lots of /s/, /ʃ/ as in 'shut' (alliteration) or lots of repeated vowels (assonance). It is also possible to retell a well-known story, using specific sounds. You can either give your learners a speech sound and ask them to start from this sound, or allow the learners to choose the sounds for purely aesthetic reasons, or because there are a lot of instances in the tale where this sound recurs. Encourage them to tell the tales in class.

4 Correcting

'Avoid telling children that they sing out of key: you may break
their vital spirit and enthusiasm and induce a lack of confidence
that will be difficult to overcome.'

Martens and Van Sull 1992

Correcting pronunciation is probably one of the most frustrating
aspects of a teacher's job. It can be counter-productive, for
systematic correction of learners' pronunciation can be a major
cause of loss of learner confidence, which is one of the reasons
why mistakes are made (other reasons being lack of will to
improve, interference from other languages, inappropriate
generalization, and fossilization).

Correction should be seen as just one aspect of an ongoing
process of improvement involving the learner. This is why
activity 4.1 asks learners to determine what, and to what extent,
they want to improve. It also means there should be no
connotation of 'sin' or inadequacy when a mistake is made.

To achieve this, highlight what the learners can do and formulate
'correction' in positive terms. Indicate that learners could be
understood *more* easily, be *more* effective in communication,
speak *more* attractively, or sound *more* British or American, for
example, instead of making negative remarks. Above all, avoid
continual hammering; this often leads to a sense of inadequacy.
Instead, correct indirectly and vary your approaches.

In this chapter I first try to get rid of wrong imprinting by a
mixture of relaxation and identification (4.2 and 4.3). Activities
4.4 and 4.5 help improve group dynamics and encourage playing
to match a model. Activities 4.6 and 4.7 appeal to the musical
brain, and again improve group dynamics. In 4.8 and 4.9 the
fear of making mistakes is tackled, and in 4.10 and 4.11 learners
have fun, but also think about their mistakes.

All of these are alternatives to purely analytical correction, but it
is probably a symbiosis of both the analytical and the non-
analytical that will succeed; the more facets of the learner's
resources that are brought into play, the better. In the case of
fossilized mistakes, for example, it often helps if learners can be
brought to understand the origin of their error, while being given
a chance to approach pronunciation with new ears and to
develop a new, richer, perception of how the language sounds
and feels.

Finally, both learners and teachers need to be patient—it is not
realistic to expect instant improvement. The learners' will to

improve is paramount; they need to discover what suits them, and accept it. Teachers need to encourage greater learner independence and practice at home. Many factors are in play, and pronunciation may need nurturing to take root. The world outside the classroom may exert a strong negative influence; the aim of this book is to help make what happens in class sufficiently interesting to carry learners along in the right direction.

4.1 Pronunciation weeding

LEVEL   **Elementary and above (except very young learners)**

TIME   **30 minutes at home or in the language laboratory + 20 minutes in class**

AIMS   **Students decide to what extent they want to 'weed out' incorrect stress, intonation, sounds, and words**

MATERIALS   **A class set of a tape with a pre-recorded text, the transcript of the text, and a questionnaire (optional)**

PREPARATION   1 Prepare a recording (if possible spoken by a native speaker) of a short text and a transcript. (You could use the tape from your coursebook.) Ideally, each student should have a copy of both (you can use a language laboratory if available).

2 **(Optional)** Prepare a questionnaire like the one on the next page. Adapt the text and questionnaire to the age and level of your learners.

PROCEDURE   1 Introduce the topic of improving pronunciation with a metaphor of a garden. Tell them there may be some 'weeds' in their pronunciation and that it would be a good idea to look at those 'weeds' and decide which ones they would like to get rid of.

2 Hand out the transcript and ask your students to record themselves reading it at home or in the language laboratory first.

3 Next lesson, ask your students to listen to the pre-recorded text and compare it with their own rendering. Ask them to decide what they would like to improve. You may find it useful to give out a questionnaire such as the one on the next page:

WEEDING OUT MY PRONUNCIATION

1 Does what I say come across clearly? If not, where is it difficult to understand?

2 Do I notice any differences between the speed of the native speaker and my own? Where?

3 Do I notice any differences between the rhythm of the native speaker and my own? Where?

4 Do I notice any differences between the intonation of the native speaker and my own? Examples?

5 Are there any particular sounds and words that I notice are different? Which ones?

6 Are there other differences? Where?

7 Which particular aspects of my pronunciation would I like to improve?

8 What do I want to achieve in my pronunciation? Basic intelligibility, or to sound as much like a native speaker as possible?

9 Have I already tried or am I trying to improve some aspects? Which ones? How? Am I satisfied with my progress?

Ask your students to bring their answers to the next lesson.

4 In the next lesson, allow your students to talk about their answers with a partner. Monitor and give advice where needed. Ask them to change partners if you see that they are interested in talking more about this.

5 Ask your students to keep a note of 'weeds' they would like to get rid of and if they believe they have found a way to eradicate them. Keep a copy of their lists. This will give you an idea of how far your students are willing to go to improve their English and what aspects you can work on with them.

6 In the coming weeks you can work on the aspects mentioned by your students, using activities from Chapters 1–3. Then do one of the follow-up activities.

FOLLOW-UP 1

After a month or so go through the activity again to see if your students feel they have improved, and if their personal view of their progress matches yours. (They should keep their original recordings and the questionnaire for comparison.) Pay particular attention to students who feel they have not improved and make them aware of points where they have improved, if possible.

FOLLOW-UP 2

After some time take another—more difficult—text to use for comparison and ask the class to provide the same kind of feedback. Tell them you are giving them more advanced work. This gives students the feeling that they are improving.

FOLLOW-UP 3

If your students are quite confident and mature, do this activity again after about a month, but ask them to appraise someone else's performance as well as their own. They discuss their findings.

FOLLOW-UP 4

If you feel it is necessary, give your own appraisal as well, but without discouraging your students.

COMMENTS

This activity makes it possible to steer your students closer towards their needs for their profession or for school exams.

4.2 Ear cleaning

LEVEL

All

TIME

5–10 minutes

AIMS

Uprooting fossilized mistakes

PREPARATION

Select the point you want to work on, and—if possible—prepare a sentence in which the students usually pronounce it correctly. (See example in the Procedure.)

PROCEDURE

1 Discuss with your students a particular word or sound that they have trouble pronouncing (the stress, any sound in the word, weak forms). Tell them they have probably got an incorrect sound in their ears and that they are going to 'clean their ears' to make room for the right pronunciation.

2 Write the word in the middle of the board and encourage your students to write it on the board or in their exercise books, in any way they like, using different styles of writing and different colours, highlighting the part of the word that is a problem.

3 Ask the students to sit comfortably and relax (see 1.1), to close their eyes, and listen to the sounds around them and to make a mental note so that they can make a list of them afterwards. You yourself listen carefully and pay particular attention to less obvious sounds: students breathing, your heartbeat, a fly in the room, a student moving a foot, a hand shifting position, dropping a handkerchief, etc.

4 After about one minute, ask your students to visualize the classroom and to open their eyes. Give them a minute or two to

write down what they heard and then ask them to tell the class. They should write down what other people heard that they did not. Tell them anything you heard that they did not. Suggest their ears were not sufficiently empty to hear the other sounds and that they should try again, in particular trying to hear their own breathing and their own heartbeat.

5 Ask your students to relax again, close their eyes, and listen. When you can see and feel the concentration, in a quiet, slow voice say, for example, 'You can see the word written on the board in your mind. Listen to your breathing. Look at the word in your mind—what colour is it? Look at this word as if it is the first time you have seen it. You cannot remember ever having heard it; it fills your ears with silence and your mind with a question mark.'

6 Pause for 15 seconds, and tell the class that in their minds they will see the words that you are going to say. Some of them will be the same colour as the first word in their mind.

7 Say your prepared sentence. For the stressed vowel in 'danger', for instance, you could say a sentence such as 'In the Bay of Biscay danger waits for sailors day and night, night and day.' Say this sentence several times, changing the speed, intonation, stress, and tone of voice. End by saying something like 'You can see "danger", you can hear it. You can see other words with the same colour. Danger waits for sailors in the Bay of Biscay. Now you know how "danger" sounds.'

8 Ask your students to visualize the word and to say it to themselves. Ask them to visualize the classroom and to open their eyes.

9 Ask the class which words have the same colour as the target sound in the original word (this should be the same sound), and to write down the words in the colours they saw them in.

Do not ask the learners to use the word immediately—wait until it comes up naturally in another lesson.

COMMENTS

When students have pronounced something wrong for a long time, they can be so 'polluted' by this pronunciation that some psychological 'cleansing' is useful. This activity can be used with fossilized mistakes that both teacher and learners recognize as a resilient problem.

4.3 That's me speaking

LEVEL	**All**
TIME	**5–10 minutes**
AIMS	**Improving the pronunciation of sounds/words, stress, and intonation patterns through internalization of the language and identification with a model**
MATERIALS	**A recording of a text at the level of your students and a class set of transcripts (both optional)**

PREPARATION Choose a recording of a short expressive text (or record a text yourself) that will leave an impression on your students; it should include sounds and words your students have found difficult to pronounce. Texts in the style of Szkutnik's *Thinking in English* or *Lyrics in English*, haiku, or limericks are very suitable. Prepare a class set of the text, preferably attractively hand-written. For very young learners take a poem or a stanza from a poem for children such as those by Brian Patten or A. A. Milne. It must be easy and short enough to learn by heart.

PROCEDURE 1 Tell your students you would like them to allow the English language to become *their* language. For this they will have to open up and allow the text they are going to hear to become *their* text. Do not tell them you aim to correct some mistakes, as this could make them self-conscious, tense, and unreceptive. Make sure they understand all the words of the text before you move to Step 2.

2 Ask your students to sit comfortably and to relax. (See 1.1 for suggestions on how to do this.) They close their eyes to avoid visual distractions and concentrate on listening. They should imagine it is they themselves who are speaking. Tell them to open up and follow what is said with their minds, their bodies, and their lips, but without speaking. It is better to stand or put the tape recorder at the back of the class, to the right, to help give this impression.

3 Play (or say) the text a couple of times. Encourage your students to make all the speech movements that go with the words they are hearing, but without actually speaking.

4 When you see that they can all do this, ask them to visualize the classroom and open their eyes. Hand out the text or help the students to write it from memory, making it look attractive. They could use colours for this. Very young learners can learn it by heart. Ask them to say it all together. Older learners move to Step 5.

5 The students read the texts to themselves, and then to partners of their choice. It is essential that you do not correct

them. Listen to their reading and make a mental note of sounds, words, stress patterns, intonation contours, etc. that still remain a problem so that you can include them in other activities.

6 Allow your students to comment on the activity if they wish.

FOLLOW-UP

1 Encourage your students to find short texts they like and record them. They could do this on their own, at home if they have tape-recorders, or in a self-access centre.

2 More advanced students can do the same with texts that they themselves write, including words and stress and intonation patterns that you would like them to work on.

Examples of texts

Those years. Those places. Those dreams. They are not here, they are not there. They are not anywhere. Where are they? Where are we?

Szkutnik 1994: 35

– To improve /ð/ as in 'those' and 'they', /əu/ as in 'those', /eɪ/ as in 'they', /eə/ as in 'there', and low falling intonation in 'those years', 'those places'. Choose the intonation that fits your interpretation of 'Where are they?'

You and your students can write texts in the same vein:

Work or walk, dream or work. Time to work. No time to walk. Live to work. Walk to dream, to live … walk or work?

– To improve /w/ as in 'work' and 'walk', /ɔ:/ as in 'walk', /ɜ:/ as in 'work', low rising intonation before commas, and low falling or high rising intonation for the question.

4.4 Hold on to the sound

LEVEL

All

TIME

5 minutes

AIMS

Correcting sounds, syllables, words, intonation contours, or stress patterns

MATERIALS

Word cards (see Preparation)

PREPARATION

Do this when students replace a sound, stress pattern, or intonation contour by another one.

1 Decide which sounds, stress patterns, or intonation contour you want to work on. Prepare lists of suitable words or short sentences to practise them. For example, if a student has a

tendency to say /ɔ:/ as in 'door' or /aʊ/ as in 'now' instead of /əʊ/ as in 'no', prepare the following words on three cards.

1	2	3
saw	sew	sow
boar	bow	bow
floor	flow	flower, flour
or	Oh	our, hour
law	low	cow

2 Make a set of cards for each three or four students.

PROCEDURE

1 Put the class in groups of about four, but put very shy learners in pairs.

2 Present this as a game. One student tries to repeat the target sound (words or phrases, sounds, stress, or intonation) accurately, no matter what the others in the group say. The others must do all they can to make the first student say one of their versions.

3 Hand out the cards and tell one student in each group (or pair) to work on the target sound in the middle column. They say the words in their column after the others have said theirs. The students with the middle column try to keep their sound consistent.

4 The fourth student acts as a 'judge' and decides whether the student in the middle is pronouncing correctly. If they are working in pairs the other student in the pair doubles as a 'judge'. Congratulate students who manage to hold on to their sound.

5 Repeat, with other students working on the target sound.

COMMENTS

Repeat this game from time to time with different target sounds (etc.). It is easy to prepare cards to work on the specific problems of individual learners.

4.5 Recognize the words

LEVEL

All except very young learners

TIME

5 minutes

AIMS

Distinguishing between similar sounds, stress patterns, and intonation

| MATERIALS | **Word cards (see Preparation)** |

PREPARATION

1 Decide which aspect of pronunciation you wish to work on. On cards or pieces of paper, write one word containing an example. You need a set for half of the class.

2 Prepare a second set of cards for the other half of the class, with a list of similar words also containing the target sound/stress/etc. You can include a couple of nonsense words. The first few words should be very different, to give confidence to the students.

If you choose to deal with stress, clearly indicate the word stress (see 2.5 for ideas on how to do this). For intonation, use sentences and draw contours above them.

Examples

a single word: thick
   list: Mick, Rick, fick, tick, thick, Vic, sick
b single word: cut
   list: cot, kt, cat, ket, cut, kit, get

c single word: expórt (as a verb)

   list: cárpet, éxport, wéather, addréss, expórt

PROCEDURE

1 Tell your students they are going to play a recognition game. Ask them to stand back to back in pairs. Student A receives a card with the single word, and student B a card with the list. They should not look at each other's cards.

2 Student B starts saying the words in the list, loud enough for student A to hear.

3 When student A thinks the word said by student B is the same as the word on his or her card, he or she stops student B and says the word. They check, and if they cannot agree, they do not look at each other's cards, but call you for help.

VARIATION 1

Put a different word on each card for the A students, or give each student B a slightly different list. They can then change partners several times and repeat the game.

VARIATION 2

Ask students to make lists of words based on their own problems. Composing the lists will make them more aware of the sounds of English and their spellings. Check the lists before you use them.

VARIATION 3

Appoint a third student as a referee, who listens to the others and says if she or he agrees. Though this student's role is more passive, real learning will ensue.

4.6 Put them in a song

LEVEL

Elementary and above

TIME

5–10 minutes

AIMS

Correcting words and sounds through singing

MATERIALS

A recording of the song (optional), a class set of the lyrics of the song and of the lyrics with blanks (see Preparation)

PREPARATION

1 Make a note of sounds or words your students pronounce less than satisfactorily.

2 Choose a song that will appeal to them and where some words can easily be replaced by others without changing the rhythm. Make enough copies of the song for your class. Prepare a second version with some words blanked out. For example, in 'My Bonnie lies over the ocean', replace 'Bonnie' with a blank each time:

> My (Bonnie) lies over the ocean
> My (Bonnie) lies over the sea
> My (Bonnie) lies over the ocean
> O bring back my (Bonnie) to me
> Bring back, bring back, O bring back my (Bonnie) to me
> Bring back, bring back, O bring back my (Bonnie) to me
> (traditional)

For young learners who cannot yet read, choose a simple song they can remember easily and do the activity orally.

PROCEDURE

1 Either play the recording of the song, or sing the song with the class. If necessary give out the lyrics.

2 Hand out the version with blanks.

3 Now ask your students to sing a sound you want to work on instead of the blank, for example:

> My /eɪ eɪ/ lies over the ocean …

4 Replace the sound with a word containing the sound (e.g. state, aim, pay-day, crazy for /eɪ/).

COMMENTS

1 Lengthen the syllable where necessary or repeat the sound to match the rhythm of the song.

2 When replacing two-syllable words make sure the stress falls on the right syllable to fit the music.

3 Your students can suggest songs to use, either in class or on their own.

Some songs you can use

Hello, goodbye (Beatles)
O my darling Clementine

Waltzing Matilda
Skye boat song
Home on the range
Shenandoah
Coming round the mountain
Come, follow.

4 Students can also practise scales with sounds and words. They can use different words and short phrases.

COMMENT

This very simple procedure generates a lot of enthusiasm. It is the enthusiasm that helps to imprint the correct pronunciation.

4.7 The sound orchestra

LEVEL

All

TIME

5–10 minutes

AIMS

Correcting pronunciation through singing

MATERIALS

Texts of a song (optional)

PREPARATION

Decide which sound(s) you want to work on. Select a suitable song, chant, or rhyme which has plenty of examples of the sound. Prepare a class set of the words if necessary. See Further Reading for collections of suitable songs.

PROCEDURE

1 Teach your class the song (or chant or rhyme), and sing it together until they know it well. Then tell them that some students will sing/say the words while others accompany by singing or saying just one sound. If you are working on consonants, make up a nonsense syllable with a consonant and a vowel, for example /dɑː/.

2 Put your students into two groups, standing in semi-circles if possible. One group will sing normally, while the 'orchestra' (the students in the other group) will accompany them by singing or saying the target sound whenever it occurs in the song. For this group you can choose students who need to improve, but do not tell them this is the reason for your choice.

3 Do this a couple of times, and then the groups can change roles.

Examples

1 'London Bridge' (Opie 1955: 76) is suitable for most age groups. Different stanzas are suitable for different sounds. The vocabulary is not uninteresting and the story behind it can lead to discussions at fairly advanced levels.

First stanza:

> London Bridge is broken down,
> Broken down, broken down,
> London Bridge is broken down,
> My fair lady.

I have used this with an 'orchestra' of /l/, /b/, /d/, /əʊ/ (show), /aʊ/ (now), /aɪ/ (my).

Third stanza:

> Wood and clay will wash away,
> Wash away, wash away,
> Wood and clay will wash away,
> My fair lady.

This is ideal for /w/ 'instruments'.

2 'Bow-wow, says the dog' (Opie 1955: 23) is particularly attractive to young learners, and enables you to insist on different vowel sounds, depending on the pupils.

> Bow-wow, says the dog,
> Mew, mew, says the cat,
> Grunt, grunt goes the hog,
> And squeak goes the rat.

> Tu-whu, says the owl,
> Caw, caw, says the crow,
> Quack, quack says the duck,
> And what cuckoos say you know.

3 I have used the following rhyme (Opie 1955: 98) to improve a variety of sounds by asking the students to change lines two and three to include words with particular sounds.

> Tommy Trot, a man of law,
> Sold his bed and lay upon straw;
> Sold the straw and slept on grass,
> To buy his wife a looking-glass.

FOLLOW-UP 1

Repeat this now and then, so that your students can gradually improve by making a better contribution to the 'orchestra'. If you hear that some students are still having problems with the sound you are practising, it is advisable to word your feedback in terms of 'improving the song' or 'playing the instrument better' rather than 'pronouncing better'.

FOLLOW-UP 2

Repeat the procedure with different sounds. Gradually increase the range of your 'orchestra' to up to five sounds.

VARIATION

You can also ask the orchestra to replace all the sounds of the song with the sound you want to practise. So, for example, following the rhythm of the song or rhyme they say /gɑ:/ for each syllable.

1 You will find suitable rhymes in *The Oxford Nursery Rhyme Book* (Opie 1955), which contains 800 rhymes. Some other collections (see Further Reading) also have recordings which you can use to provide a model for learners. Some (such as Buck 1984) also have musical scores, and you can encourage musical learners to play them in class. Many old rhymes exist in several versions; if you have more than one you can use them to develop your learners' generative abilities.

2 In this activity modelling is provided by the other members of the 'orchestra'. Learners have an opportunity to try again and again without being exposed to the scrutiny of the teacher and the other students all the time.

4.8 Try at least twice

LEVEL

All

TIME

5 minutes

AIMS

Overcoming fear of making mistakes

PROCEDURE

1 Tell your students that we often make mistakes out of sheer fear of making them. We hardly ever get something right when we try to get it right, so you have decided to forbid them to do it right first time. Tell them you want them to get it right after three attempts—as a concession you might accept them getting it right the second time!

2 Pair your students up and ask them to practise pronouncing a word, sentence, etc. Their partners must make a note of when they get it right.

3 They change partners and repeat.

4 Ask who managed to get it right the third time, the second time, and the first time.

COMMENTS

1 This approach is particularly effective when students are so afraid to make mistakes that they avoid speaking. It gets rid of the anxiety caused by the pressure to get it right, and actually helps learners to do so the first time!

2 It may be worth always allowing your students to try anything they have just learnt twice.

4.9 Say what you can or what you can't

LEVEL   **All**

TIME   **5 minutes**

AIMS   **Correcting the pronunciation of particular English sounds**

PROCEDURE

1 Choose a sound your students have difficulty pronouncing, for example /θ/ (th). Give them permission to instead pronounce another, very different sound you know they find easy. For example, instead of /θ/, say /p/ or /m/. Try to have the sound in different positions in your practice sentences. So they will say:

Mank you for coming.
I need a bam. /ba:m/
What on earp!
I pink pree pings are missing.
Arpur eats anyping.

2 Then ask them to pronounce the sound they usually confuse /θ/ with—/s/, /f/, and /t/ are the most common ones. This helps them to become aware that what they pronounce is different from what it should be.

3 Next, ask your students not to pronounce a sound at all:

Ank you for coming.
I need a ba.
What on ear!
I ink ree ings are missing.
Ar ur eats any ing.

4 Now allow the students to pronounce /θ/ or not, as they wish. Do not comment on their performance.

5 Finally, ask them to say the sentences with the correct sounds.

VARIATION

The reverse can also be effective: ask your students to only pronounce the difficult sounds, remaining silent for the rest of the word or sentence. Not having to worry about the rest often helps.

COMMENTS

With 'difficult' words or sentences it can help at first to let students just say the parts they feel confident with, but keeping to the rhythm and stress of the word or sentence. Then they can gradually work up to saying the whole.

4.10 Pronunciation game

LEVEL	All learners who can read English
TIME	10–15 minutes
AIMS	Improving the pronunciation of words (phonemes or stress)
MATERIALS	Two sets of cards for each group (see Preparation)
PREPARATION	Prepare two sets of cards for each group of four learners, one with 'forfeits': sentences, short rhymes, proverbs, tongue twisters, or titles of songs—some they already know and others they do not. On the other set (preferably of another colour) write words some of your students do not find easy to pronounce, or that you want to practise. You can indicate sentence stress and intonation on the forfeit cards.
PROCEDURE	1 Put the learners in groups of up to four and give out the sets of cards face down on the table. Each group decides who will begin. The others follow, going clockwise.
	2 The first student takes the card at the top of the 'words' pack and reads it aloud. If the group is satisfied with the pronunciation, the student puts the card back at the bottom of the pile and gets one point. If the group is not satisfied, they correct the student, who must also take the top card from the 'forfeits' pile and read out what is on it. (If it is a song title they have to sing the song.) If there are disagreements about the pronunciation of the word card, allow the students to check their notes or in a dictionary or to ask you. Monitor carefully and make a note of words that the students still find difficult. The other students take their turns.
	3 After about 5 to 10 minutes, the points are counted up.
	4 Working with the whole class, write two or three words that are still mispronounced on the board. Silently point at one and invite students to pronounce it. Ask them to prepare a two-line rhyme containing those words for the next lesson.
	5 Next lesson, ask the students to say their two-line rhymes. The class vote for the 'best' one.
VARIATION	If you are trying to associate two similar sounds with their spellings, for instance /ɔː/ as in (door) and /əʊ/ as in (show), prepare a set of cards with words containing different spellings of the sounds, e.g. source, sauce, saw, and so, sow, though.
	1 Put your students in groups of four and give each group a pack of word cards.
	2 On the board, write a pair of words with the sounds you want to work on, for instance: 'door' and 'dough', and number them (1) and (2).

3 In turn, students take a card from the set and pronounce the word on it, also saying which sound they think it is.

Example: 'dawn'—number one.

4 If the group agrees, nobody challenges the answer and the student gets a point. If someone challenges, the one who is wrong loses a point and the one who is right wins one. Stop the game after a maximum of 10 minutes. The student in the group who has the most points wins.

4.11 William Wombat

LEVEL   **Any learners who can read English**

TIME   **10 minutes**

AIMS   **Correcting sounds, sound combinations, words, stress patterns, intonation contours, etc.**

MATERIALS   **Lists of words, phrases, or clauses containing the point you wish to focus on**

PREPARATION   On the board or on sheets of paper, write several lists of words or phrases at your students' level containing the problem you wish to work on. Whenever possible do this with your students. You should have as many items as there are students in the class. (If your class is very large, you can divide it into groups to play the game either simultaneously or at different times.) It is best to have several lists, so that students can swap sheets after a while. Adapt the example opposite to suit your classes.

For /w/ the following list could be used. You could use lists with nouns, verbs, or adjectives only at first and add more word classes later. Make up a striking name that contains the sound you want to work on. For /w/ I have chosen 'William Wombat'.

Nouns	Verbs	Adjectives	Others
wind	wish	wan	what
water	want	windy	when
wish	work	white	why
wage	wait	warm	where
wolf	walk	wary	while
walk	waltz	washy	with
wake	wander	waste	Walter
wall	wonder	wavy	Wilma
wallet	wane	weak	Wilfred
will	warn	weird	Wendy
walnut	wash	well	
waltz	wear	Welsh	
war	weave	winter	
war-cry	wed	wide	
watch	weed	wild	
wave	weigh	wiry	
way	weep	wise	
weasel	win	witty	
weather	whisk	wooded	

Photocopiable © Oxford University Press

PROCEDURE

1 Put up the list on the board or hand it out. Make sure the learners understand all the words, including 'wombat'. Assign each student a word from the first column. Pronounce the words as you assign them.

2 Tell them they will have to react quickly when they hear the word that has been assigned to them, and make up a sentence containing at least one of the words from the first column and as many words from the other columns as they can.

3 You begin: for example, 'William Wombat wants to eat winter walnuts.'

The student who has been assigned 'walnut' must react instantly and make up a sentence such as 'William Wombat does not want to eat winter walnuts, William Wombat wants to buy a wallet.' The 'wallet' student goes on: 'William Wombat does not want to buy a wallet, he wants to waltz with Wendy.' and so on.

4 Observe and listen carefully. If you notice that there is still a problem with the point you are focusing on, stop the activity after a short time and try it again in another lesson after some more practice using any suitable activity from Chapters 2 or 3, or possibly some more analytical work.

5 Otherwise, continue until everyone has had a go. The class vote for the funniest sentence.

6 If you believe the students can pronounce the target sound

better than they did during the game, you can simply ask them to read a couple of words of their choice from the list, and praise them if they manage to say them correctly.

VARIATION

To 'correct' students who confuse two sounds such as /æ/ as in 'bad' and /ʌ/ as in 'shut', for example, use 'William Wombat' in the following way.

1 Prepare a list with three columns as in the main Procedure. The first column should alternate words with /æ/ and words with /ʌ/. The second column contains only /æ/ words, and the third only /ʌ/ words. When the students make new sentences, they should always use words that contain the same sound as in the word assigned to them.

2 Then ask them to use words that have the other sound.

3 As your students improve, use only two columns: one as before, and another where the two sounds are mixed.

Acknowledgements

This game is derived from 'Pancho Carrancho', a game invented by Ramiro Garcia (1985) to practise vocabulary and structures. Here it has been adapted to improve pronunciation. It is easy to find more variations to suit your students.

Bibliography

Alahuhta, E. 1980. 'On the primary factors predicting linguistic abilities in preschool children.' *Proceedings of the First International Congress of the Study of Child Language.*

Alahuhta, E. 1986. 'Les problèmes des écoliers qui ne savent pas écouter.' *Bulletin d'audiophonologie—annales scientifiques de l'université de Franche-Comté* 2/5&6: 615–22.

Anderson-Hsieh, J. 1992. 'Using electronic feedback to teach suprasegmentals.' *System* 20/1: 51–62.

Aucher, M-L. 1977. *L'Homme sonore.* Paris: Epi.

Auriol, B. 1991. *La Clef des sons: éléments de psychosonique.* Toulouse: Erès.

Cabrera Abreu, M. and **J. A. Maidment.** 1993. 'An Analysis of the Effects of Voice Variation on Pause and Voice Duration in English and Spanish.' *Speech Hearing and Language: Work in Progress* 7: 43–51 London: University College Department of Phonetics and Linguistics.

Davis, P. and **M. Rinvolucri.** 1988. *Dictation: New Methods, New Possibilities.* Cambridge: Cambridge University Press.

Davis, P. and **M. Rinvolucri.** 1990. *The Confidence Book.* Harlow: Longman.

Dufeu, B. 1992. *Sur les chemins d'une pédagogie de l'être.* Mainz: Editions Dramaturgie.
This is the original, more complete version of:

Dufeu, B. 1994. *Teaching Myself.* Oxford: Oxford University Press.

Estienne, F. 1993. *Je suis bien dans ma voix.* Brussels: Office Central de Librairie.

Crystal , D. 1986. 'Prosodic Development' in P. Fletcher and M. Garman (eds.): *Language Acquisition: Studies in First Language Development.* Cambridge: Cambridge University Press.

Garcia, R. 1985. *Instructor's Notebook: How to Apply TPR For Best Results.* Los Gatos, Calif.: Sky Oaks Productions.

Hadfield, J. 1992. *Classroom Dynamics.* Oxford: Oxford University Press. Resource Books for Teachers series.

Kermani, K. 1992. *Autogenic Training: New Way to Beat Stress Successfully.* London: Thorsons.

Krnic, B. and **M. Wambach.** 1989. 'De la rhythmique corporelle et musicale à la correction phonétique dans un cours de langues destiné aux adultes.' *Bulletin du CIAVER* 57: 38–56.

Malfait, R. 1980. *Progressieve Relaxatie en Autogene Training: Basismethode voor het Leren Ontspannen.* Leuven (Belgium): Acco.

Martens, E. and **V. Van Sull.** 1992. *Oser la musique!* Brussels: Labor.

Molholt, G. 1988. 'Computer-Assisted Instruction in

Pronunciation for Chinese Speakers of American English.' in *TESOL Quarterly* 22(1): 91–111.

Morgan, J. and **M. Rinvolucri.** 1983. *Once Upon a Time.* Cambridge: Cambridge University Press.

Moskowitz, G. 1978. *Caring and Sharing in the Language Classroom.* Rowley, Mass.: Newbury House.

Porter-Ladousse, G. 1987. *Role Play.* Oxford: Oxford University Press. Resource Books for Teachers series.

Schultz, J. H. 1956. *Das autogene Training: konzentrative Selbstenspannung, Versuch einer klinisch-praktischen Darstellung.* Stuttgart: Thieme.

Szkutnik, L. L. 1993. *Lyrics in English.* Warsaw: Wiedza Powszechna. Cassette also available.

Szkutnik, L. L. 1994 (new edition). *Thinking in English.* Warsaw: Veda.

Tomatis, A. 1991 (new edition). *L'Oreille et le langage.* Paris: Seuil. Originally published in 1963.

Tomatis, A. 1977. *L'Oreille et la vie.* Paris: Laffont.

Tomatis, A. 1987. *L'Oreille et la voix.* Paris: Laffont.
Quite a few of Tomatis's ideas need to taken with caution, but he deserves credit for highlighting the importance of the child's contact with the human voice before birth.

Wessels, C. 1987. *Drama.* Oxford: Oxford University Press. Resource Books for Teachers series.

Williams, L. V. 1983. *Teaching for the Two-sided Mind.* Englewood Cliffs: Prentice Hall.

Further reading

1 Collections of verse and songs

Belloc, H. 1993. *Selected Cautionary Verses.* London: Jonathan Cape and Harmondsworth: Penguin.

Belloc, H. 1992. *Cautionary Verses.* Two cassettes read by Stephen Fry. New York: Random House.

Betjeman, J. 1979. *Collected Poems.* London: John Murray. Collections also published by Penguin.

Buck, P. 1984. *The Oxford Nursery Song Book.* Oxford: Oxford University Press.

Burgess, G. 1900. *Goops and How to Be Them.* New York: reprinted by Dover Books, 1969.

Carroll, L. 1960. *The Humorous Verse of Lewis Carroll.* New York: Dover Books.

Cass-Beggs, R. 1982. *The Penguin Book of Rounds.* Harmondsworth: Penguin.

Graham, C. 1979. *Jazz Chants for Children.* Oxford: Oxford University Press. (Student's book, Teacher's book, Cassette)

Graham, C. 1984. *Small Talk: More Jazz Chants*. Oxford: Oxford University Press. For adults.

Grigson, G. 1982. *The Faber Book of Nonsense Verse*. London: Faber and Faber.

Laing, R. D. 1970. *Knots*. London: Tavistock. (Also published in 1971 by Penguin.)

Lear, E. 1984. *The Complete Nonsense of Edward Lear*. London: Faber and Faber.

Lear, E. 1993. *Nonsense Songs*. Basingstoke: Macmillan.

Milne, A. A. 1991. *Pooh's Poems*. London: Methuen.

Milne, A. A. 1994. *Poems and Hums of Pooh*. London: Methuen.

Nash, O. 1975. *'I Wouldn't have Missed it': Selected Poems of Ogden Nash*. Boston and Toronto: Little, Brown, and Company.

Opie, I. and **P. Opie.** 1951. *The Oxford Dictionary of Nursery Rhymes*. Oxford: Oxford University Press.

Opie, I. and **P. Opie.** 1955. *The Oxford Nursery Rhyme Book*. Oxford: Oxford University Press.

Opie, I. and **P. Opie.** 1973. *The Oxford Book of Children's Verse*. Oxford: Oxford University Press.

Opie, I. and **P. Opie.** 1985. *The Singing Game*. Oxford: Oxford University Press.

Patten, B. 1985. *Gargling with Jelly*. London: Viking and Harmondsworth: Penguin.

Patten, B. 1990. *Thawing Frozen Frogs*. London: Viking and Harmondsworth: Penguin.

Sissay, L. 1988. *Tender Fingers in a Clenched Fist*. London: Bogle L'Ouverture.

Vaughan-Rees, M. (ed.) 1992. *Rhymes and Rhythm*. Whitstable, Kent: IATEFL. Special issue of *Speak Out*, the newsletter of the International Association of Teachers of English as a Foreign Language Pronunciation Special Interest Group. Cassette available.

Watson, J. 1979. *The Children's Book of Funny Verse*. London: Guild Publishing.

2 Collections of tales

Foss, M. 1977. *Folk Tales of the British Isles*. London: Book Club Associates.

Lang, A. 1975. *The Blue Fairy Book*. Harmondsworth: Penguin.

O'Faolain, E. 1965. *Children of the Salmon and other Irish Folktales*. London: Longman.

Opie, I. and **P. Opie.** 1974. *Classic Fairy Tales*. Oxford: Oxford University Press.

Wright, A. 1995. *Storytelling with Children*. Oxford: Oxford University Press. Resource Books for Teachers series.

3 Pronunciation 'basics'

Adams, C. 1979. *English Speech Rhythm and the Foreign Learner.* The Hague: Mouton.

Avery, P. and **S. Ehrlich.** 1992. *Teaching American English Pronunciation.* Oxford: Oxford University Press.

Bolinger, D. 1972. 'Accent is predictable (if you're a mind reader).' *Language* 48/3: 633–44.

Bolinger, D. 1986. *Intonation and its Parts.* London: Edward Arnold.

Bolinger, D. 1989. *Intonation and its Uses: Melody in Grammar and Discourse.* London: Edward Arnold.

Brazil, D. 1985. *The Communicative Value of Intonation in English.* Birmingham: English Language Research (University of Birmingham).

Brown, A. (ed.). 1992. *Approaches to Pronunciation Teaching.* Basingstoke: Macmillan.

Catford, J. C. 1988. *A Practical Introduction to Phonetics.* Oxford: Oxford University Press.

Cruttenden, A. 1986. *Intonation.* Cambridge: Cambridge University Press.

Crystal, D. 1969. *Prosodic Systems and Intonation in English.* Cambridge: Cambridge University Press.

Dalton, C. and **B. Seidlhofer,** 1994. *Pronunciation.* Oxford: Oxford University Press. Scheme for Teacher Education series.

De Bot, C. L. J. 1982. *Visuele Feedback van Intonatie.* Enschede: Sneldruk Boulevard Diss. Doctor in de letteren (Katholieke Universiteit te Nijmegen).

Esling, J. H. 1985. 'Voice quality settings and the teaching of pronunciation.' *TESOL Quarterly* 17/1: 89–95.

Gimson, A. C. and **A. Cruttenden.** 1994 (new edition). *An Introduction to the Pronunciation of English.* London: Edward Arnold.

Helmholtz, H. 1954. *On the Sensations of Tone.* New York: Dover. (Originally pubished in1885 as *Die Lehre von den Tonempfindungen.*)

Honikman, B. 1964. 'Articulatory settings' in D. Abercrombie (ed.): *In Honour of Daniel Jones.* London: Longman: 73–84.

Kenworthy, J. 1987. *Teaching English Pronunciation.* Harlow: Longman.

Ladefoged, P. 1993. *A Course in Phonetics.* Fort Worth: Harcourt Brace Jovanovich.

McCallion, M. 1988. *The Voice Book.* London: Faber and Faber.

Pennington, M. C. and **J. C. Richards.** 1986. 'Pronunciation revisited.' *TESOL Quarterly* 20/2: 207–25.

Porter, D. and **S. Garvin.** 1989. 'Attitudes to pronunciation in EFL.' *Speak Out!* 5: 8–15.

Renard, R. 1971. *Introduction à la méthode verbo-tonale de correction phonétique.* Paris and Brussels: Didier Édition Internationale.

Roach, P. 1983. *English Phonetics and Phonology*. Cambridge: Cambridge University Press.

Stevick, E. W. 1978. 'Toward a practical philosophy of pronunciation: another view.' *TESOL Quarterly* 12/2: 145–50.

Woodward, T. 1991. 'Making stress physical, visible and audible.' *MET* 17/3&4: 38–9

4 Background reading

Bachmann, M-L. 1992. 'Musik und Körper.' *Rhythmik* 2: 38–44.

Delbe, A. 1991. 'L'image du corps vocale.' *Pratique des mots* 75: 2–8.

Horwitz, E. K. and **D. J. Young.** 1991. *Language Anxiety: From Theory and Research to Classroom Implications*. Englewood Cliffs: Prentice Hall.

Jackendoff, R. 1987. *Consciousness and the Computational Mind*. Cambridge, Mass.: M.I.T. Press.

Jousse, M. 1969. *L'Anthropologie du Geste*. Paris: Resma.

Kreiman, J. et al. 1993. 'Perceptual evaluation of voice quality: review, tutorial and a framework for future research.' *Journal of Speech and Hearing Research* 36: 21–40.

Marc, P. 1991. *Autour de la notion pédagogique d'attente*. Berne: Peter Lang.

Moore, B. C. J. 1982. *An Introduction to the Psychology of Hearing*. London: Academic Press.

Richmond, V. P., J. C. McCroskey, and **S. K. Payne.** 1987. *Nonverbal Behavior in Interpersonal Relations*. Englewood Cliffs, N.J.: Prentice Hall.

Sebeok, T. A. and **D. Umiker-Sebeok (eds.).** 1976. *Speech Surrogates: Drum and Whistle Systems*. The Hague: Mouton.

Simon, S., L. W. Howe, and **H. Kirschenbaum.** 1972. *Values Clarification: A Handbook of Practical Strategies for Teachers and Students*. New York: Hart Publishing Co./Dodd and Mead.

Stein, B. and **A. Meredith.** 1993. *The Merging of the Senses*. Cambridge, Mass.: MIT Press.

Uhde, D. 1976. *Listening and Voice—A Phenomenology of Sound*. Athens, Ohio: Ohio University Press.

Van Eeckhout, P. and **P. Bhatt.** 1984. 'Rythme, intonation, accentuation: la rééducation des aphasies non fluentes sévères.' *Rééducation Orthophonique* 22/138): 311–27.

Van Lancker, D. and **J. Sidtis.** 1992. 'The identification of affective-prosodic stimuli by left- and right-hemisphere-damaged subjects: all errors are not created equal.' *Journal of Speech and Hearing Research* 35/5: 963–70.

Appendix

Phonemic symbols

Vowels and diphthongs

1	iː	as in	**see** /siː/	11	ɜː	as in	**fur** /fɜː(r)/
2	ɪ	as in	**sit** /sɪt/	12	ə	as in	**ago** /əˈgəʊ/
3	e	as in	**ten** /ten/	13	eɪ	as in	**page** /peɪdʒ/
4	æ	as in	**hat** /hæt/	14	əʊ	as in	**home** /həʊm/
5	ɑː	as in	**arm** /ɑːm/	15	aɪ	as in	**five** /faɪv/
6	ɒ	as in	**got** /gɒt/	16	aʊ	as in	**now** /naʊ/
7	ɔː	as in	**saw** /sɔː/	17	ɔɪ	as in	**join** /dʒɔɪn/
8	ʊ	as in	**put** /pʊt/	18	ɪə	as in	**near** /nɪə(r)/
9	uː	as in	**too** /tuː/	19	eə	as in	**hair** /heə(r)/
10	ʌ	as in	**cup** /kʌp/	20	ʊə	as in	**pure** /pjʊə(r)/

Consonants

1	p	as in	**pen** /pen/	13	s	as in	**so** /səʊ/
2	b	as in	**bad** /bæd/	14	z	as in	**zoo** /zuː/
3	t	as in	**tea** /tiː/	15	ʃ	as in	**she** /ʃiː/
4	d	as in	**did** /dɪd/	16	ʒ	as in	**vision** /ˈvɪʒn/
5	k	as in	**cat** /kæt/	17	h	as in	**how** /haʊ/
6	g	as in	**got** /gɒt/	18	m	as in	**man** /mæn/
7	tʃ	as in	**chin** /tʃɪn/	19	n	as in	**no** /nəʊ/
8	dʒ	as in	**June** /dʒuːn/	20	ŋ	as in	**sing** /sɪŋ/
9	f	as in	**fall** /fɔːl/	21	l	as in	**leg** /leg/
10	v	as in	**voice** /vɔɪs/	22	r	as in	**red** /red/
11	θ	as in	**thin** /θɪn/	23	j	as in	**yes** /jes/
12	ð	as in	**then** /ðen/	24	w	as in	**wet** /wet/

/ˈ/ represents primary stress as in **about** /əˈbaʊt/

Index